Journalism from Print to Platform

Through a synthesis of philosophical anthropology and media theory, this book examines the human relationship with technology, progressing from analogue to digital, to give a new perspective on journalism in the digital age.

Journalism from Print to Platform takes a fresh look at the relationship between journalism as a craft shaped by its tools and considers anew the tools themselves. This book demonstrates that, with the emergence of digitality, what analogue print culture made possible and seemingly "natural" has now become unworkable. Digital logic constitutes a wholly different category of technology with a framework that makes fidelity in one-to-one exchange of analogue-to-digital in communication problematic. In short, the technology-based forms and practices that journalism developed as a fourth estate/public sphere enabler are, like us, irreducibly analog. Whilst we have mostly assumed that these would either adapt to or carry over with the shift to digitality, this book challenges that assumption and considers the important consequences of that realisation for the practice of journalism today.

This challenging study is an insightful resource for students and scholars in journalism, media and technology studies.

Robert Hassan is Professor of Media and Communication at the University of Melbourne, Australia.

Disruptions: Studies in Digital Journalism
Series editor: Bob Franklin

Disruptions refers to the radical changes provoked by the affordances of digital technologies that occur at a pace and on a scale that disrupts settled understandings and traditional ways of creating value, interacting and communicating both socially and professionally. The consequences for digital journalism involve far reaching changes to business models, professional practices, roles, ethics, products and even challenges to the accepted definitions and understandings of journalism. For Digital Journalism Studies, the field of academic inquiry that explores and examines digital journalism, disruption results in paradigmatic and tectonic shifts in scholarly concerns. It prompts reconsideration of research methods, theoretical analyses and responses (oppositional and consensual) to such changes, which have been described as being akin to "a moment of mind-blowing uncertainty".

Routledge's book series, *Disruptions: Studies in Digital Journalism*, seeks to capture, examine and analyse these moments of exciting and explosive professional and scholarly innovation that characterise developments in the day-to-day practice of journalism in an age of digital media and which are articulated in the newly emerging academic discipline of Digital Journalism Studies.

Algorithmic Gatekeeping for Professional Communicators
Power, Trust and Legitimacy
Arjen van Dalen

The Disputed Freedoms of a Disrupted Press
Ivor Shapiro

Reviving Rural News
Transforming the Business Model of Community Journalism in the US and Beyond
Teri Finneman, Nick Mathews and Patrick Ferrucci

Journalism from Print to Platform
The Impossible Shift from Analog to Digital?
Robert Hassan

For more information about this series, please visit: www.routledge.com/Disruptions/book-series/DISRUPTDIGJOUR

Journalism from Print to Platform

The Impossible Shift from Analog to Digital

Robert Hassan

LONDON AND NEW YORK

First published 2024
by Routledge
4 Park Square, Milton Park, Abingdon, Oxon OX14 4RN

and by Routledge
605 Third Avenue, New York, NY 10158

Routledge is an imprint of the Taylor & Francis Group, an informa business

British Library Cataloguing-in-Publication Data
A catalogue record for this book is available from the British Library

Library of Congress Cataloging-in-Publication Data
Names: Hassan, Robert, 1959- author.
Title: Journalism from print to platform: the impossible shift from analog to digital / Robert Hassan.
Description: London; New York: Routledge, 2024. |
Series: Disruptions: studies in digital journalism |
Includes bibliographical references and index.
Identifiers: LCCN 2024004040 (print) | LCCN 2024004041 (ebook) | ISBN 9780367515133 (hardback) | ISBN 9781003054207 (paperback) | ISBN 9780367515140 (ebook)
Subjects: LCSH: Journalism–Technological innovations. | Philosophical anthropology.
Classification: LCC PN4784.T34 H37 2024 (print) | LCC PN4784.T34 (ebook) | DDC 070.43–dc23/eng/20240130
LC record available at https://lccn.loc.gov/2024004040
LC ebook record available at https://lccn.loc.gov/2024004041

ISBN: 9780367515133 (hbk)
ISBN: 9780367515140 (pbk)
ISBN: 9781003054207 (ebk)

DOI: 10.4324/9781003054207

Typeset in Times New Roman
by Deanta Global Publishing Services, Chennai, India

Contents

Introduction

Journalism is still modern (and that is a problem)

The approaching death of journalism is a trope that has been around for several turbulent decades now. During that time the reasons for its demise have been the subject of many inquisitions and treatises from many sources. Social democratic governments have launched inquiries into the "future of public interest journalism" (Australian Senate Committee, 2017); illiberal regimes have exploited the profession's relative weakness as an opportunity to manipulate and control it (Polyák, 2019); university research centres have studied the vocation as an endangered "historical-political practice" (Polis, 2023); myriad academics have written angst-filled books on how journalism must rage against the dying of the light (e.g. McChesney and Nichols, 2010); and journalists themselves are still busy identifying and strategizing ways and means to avert the "threats" and "risks" to their profession (Andreotti, 2015).

Causes are often seen as structural-economic, such as the 1980s emergence of neoliberal globalisation, a deeply transformative process of time-space "compression" that blurred the lingering local-national distinctions and the public spheres journalism helped form. The structural is also the technological, with journalism acting as synecdoche for a "media" made unrecognisable by digital technology—most particularly the Internet and all that is connectable to it. Such approaches have their individual merits. However, something more interesting and more illuminating emerges when the effects of globalisation and information technology are considered in combination. One could not have developed in the way it did without the other and their interaction brought each to a peak of transformative power—especially the computer (Hassan, 2020). In the mid-20th century, computing lumbered through research and administration departments in the military and in large corporations in the form of analog or analog-digital hybrid systems that were invisible to most people. Globalisation in the 1080s changed that, and the imperatives of commercialised, flexible and ultimately individualised "solutions" for practically anything brought digital processes into the lives of billions in a very visible way. However, the human consequences of such a rapid

DOI: 10.4324/9781003054207-1

and concentrated transformation from analog to digital has been relatively overlooked—due in no small part to the ideology of the neoliberal globalisation that promoted it. Today, digital technology, or digital logic, constitutes a new category of technology and constitutes a new relationship with technology that we are only just beginning to realise in terms of the profound nature of the changes it has wrought. Some of these are positive for humanity. Others are less so. But we barely understand the workings of the Internet, and its dispositions through social media and AI are conducted as a human experiment.

The long years of neoliberalism's *idée fixe* meant that the nature of digital technology has been viewed through a very narrow commercial lens. The philosophical aspects of the question have been largely sidelined. Attempts were made during the 1980s and 1990s to think more philosophically about what was being lost to the digital tsunami then just getting underway (e.g., Postman, 1985; Roszak, 1986; Wilder, 1997). However, these gained relatively little traction amid the hyperbolic boosterism that told us computers were a solution in search of a problem.

But there was another reason why we did not pay enough attention to more reflective questions. The human relationship with a new category of technology was something we had not needed to consider before—because *analog* was all there was. And there was nothing to compare it with. Philosophically speaking, even when digital arrived, where humans stood in relation to analog and digital just did not readily suggest itself—especially to the designers of computers, software, cellphones and innumerable applications who were always focused on practical-commercial outcomes. Today the question is urgent. It is urgent because the world around us swirls in rapid and constant change, yet we humans remain the same, dazed by change and constantly trying to adapt and keep up. We speak here of journalism, but the point applies more generally—to us as *Homo sapiens*, as nature's foremost technology creators and users. It applies at the philosophical and at the *anthropological* levels, too. And so a consideration of the human-technology relation will help us understand analog and digital technology and better comprehend the world we find ourselves in—one in which journalism has no obvious place.

So, let us begin with an example, with digital and with writing, in particularl—the central journalistic skill. There is an autocorrect function in Microsoft Outlook 365, an application with some 345 million users (Redmond, 2023), whereby if you sign-off an email with the words "let's keep in touch", Microsoft has tweaked its algorithm to "correct" this apparently doubtful phrase with the suggestion "let's stay connected", instead. For some, if they trouble themselves to consider it, this may appear as just another little "efficiency" in the broad sweep of productive elements brought to our increasingly creative and dynamic lives through computers. Computers help us to write better, you might say. Another way of looking at it is that the programme wants to write *for you*, or think *for you* or change your opinion on things, even about apparently minor things like an email sign-off. And autocorrect is at only the very modest end of what AI can do. The latest algorithmic language models make it possible for you to never have to write again, with the ever-scrutinising, ever-listening computer able to take real-time dictation better and faster than most humans.

Continuing with the autocorrect function: you can ignore it or you can go with its algorithmic flow. It is your choice, or so it is said. But if you think about it in the context of our hypothesis, of the understanding of the human-technology relationship, then the example *is* significant. It helps understand how the transition from analog to digital has affected, perhaps terminally, what journalism is and what journalism does.

So, what is going on when an algorithm interrupts the flow of writing, offering unasked-for opinion on your grammar and syntax? Well, ostensibly, the suggestion "let's stay connected" instead of "let's stay in touch" may be read as harmless; a difference without a distinction, and the responsive algorithm simply optimising our writing and keeping it up to date. And to "stay connected" has obvious connotations with the media we are using—with word processing on the Internet. And the Internet, as Mark Zuckerberg CEO of Meta, never tires of stating, is about the connections that bring us together, all speaking the same language and all on the same (virtual) page, a computer-generated "community". Ok, but what's wrong with "let's stay in touch"? Why would the algorithm put its virtual hand on yours as you type and say, in effect: "do you *really* want to say that"? Staying in "touch" signifies the physical. When we write "touch" we do not necessarily mean "let's meet up and have coffee, tomorrow". The word is a hangover from another age, an age of analog communication where the objective of much correspondence was to actually "touch" at some point; goodbye till we meet (physically) again. There is a human-to-human commitment there, a carry-over from the social contract of letter writing. To "stay connected", by contrast, doesn't mean anything analog at all. It doesn't really mean anything. The imputed connection is virtual in the form of an electrical signal, digital pulses of data, down a cable or from a Wi-Fi source. This is connecting through channels that are open and available, and, as we are all potentially connected 24/7 anyway, the verb "stay" is redundant. And no commitment, no social contract, is implied.

What I'm suggesting is that human culture(s) are changing because technology is changing. And change is expressed through digital technology. Often, the change seems negligible (like autocorrect), or it goes unnoticed altogether (like autocorrect). But it matters, nonetheless. It matters because metaphors matter (Lakoff & Johnson, 1980). Metaphors feed the narratives that become the stories that we write, read, print and share to make sense of the world. By changing the metaphors, we change our awareness of the world in subtle or in fundamental ways. To move from "touch" to "connect", via Microsoft, is both subtle and fundamental. It signals a subtle shift from analog to digital that also expresses a fundamental transformation in how humans increasingly relate to one another: *virtually*. The shift is all around us in ways that are unnecessary to restate much because most of us have either experienced the shift, or we were born into an established digital culture.

Nonetheless, the analog world is still here: looming like a shadow from the past, an unfocused apparition that is the "real" world beyond the screens we stare at. But the analog world of people and mediated lives looks different now because it too has been transformed by digital. We see it in the commute to work, for instance. Not so long ago many passengers on a bus or train would be reading a newspaper or a book or magazine or perhaps speaking with someone next to them. Now almost all are looking at text, photos, video, CGI and animation on their phones—or they gaze to the middle distance as they speak to a virtual, disembodied, presence via earphones. The digital connection not only changes our relationship to each other, but also changes our relationship to the analog world we can never escape.

The print media example is apposite because the transformation of a centuries-old practice, something that has disappeared in the lifetime of millions, has been seen mostly as an inexorable economic process, as technological progress, and so just as in any other walk of life, people need to adapt. Media habits change, the industry changes, and so the forms and processes of modern journalism should change, too. Or so we are told. However, the historical-political practice of journalism is different. I will argue that it is indeed unique in a historical-political sense and is something we cannot afford to dismiss as simply the cost of progress—because in this case the colonisation by digital is not progress; it is a regression of what journalism helped to bring about as an element of the actual human progress (of a Western kind) that was the Enlightenment, the birth of mass print media, liberal democracy, modernity and the public sphere. We cannot simply graft these onto a new category of media technology without asking fundamental philosophical questions.

We have been changed by digital technology. But our relationship with technology per se goes deeper than we normally imagine, and this is where anthropology meets philosophy in the form of "philosophical anthropology" (Gehlen, 1980). This perspective explores the relationship between body, mind and technology. The argument is developed in some depth below, but the essence of it is that *humans are technology*, and that is why we can transform the world in ways that no other species can—for good or ill. And that technology is *analog*. Moreover, *we* are analog (Hassan, 2023). This is how (and why) we evolved and flourished and were able to create the analog technology of writing as an extension of our thoughts. This changed how our minds worked in relation to the cultures of orality that had been our lot for thousands of years prior to the invention of writing (Ong, 1982). Writing changed how we thought and saw the world in relation to ourselves. Writing formed the basis for civilisation. And thought mechanised into print, via the Renaissance, became the foundation upon which modernity would emerge—with its distinctive conceptions of truth. Print's awesome power was that something could be accepted as "true" because it was printed (Ong, 1982, p.

77). Modernity and journalism are deeply connected in this historical-political respect. And journalism in this classical sense is *indissolubly modern.*

Digital has superseded both analog and modernity. But we are still analog beings in a world that is not ours; yet, we regard ourselves as somehow still "modern". In our digital postmodernity, the machines we created and let loose have their own "thinking": an automated logic that is too fast for us, too instrumental for us, exploits us and alienates us from our analog essence. We cannot be modern any longer. We cannot easily do what we once did, think what we once thought or see what we once saw. Digital communication changed all that. Printed words were fixed, and digital text is mutable. This phrase means a great deal in matters of truth. But journalism, at its ethical core, in its sense of itself as a profession and as a craft "remains the same" as Mark Deuze (2019, p. 2) reminds us—stranded in a "quagmire" of postmodernity. That's a problem for journalism, and it's also problem for what used to be its publics.

1 Technology and the journalist

To understand the existential moment that journalism experiences today because of digital technology, we need to look beyond the standard reasons offered—by employers, by politicians and by sundry economists. We need to think more critically about the clichés of technological "progress" and the "disruptive" effects of digital technologies that cause "unavoidable" job losses and the extensive automation of the news media industry. We need to question the lack of vision of liberal politicians, of tech industry bosses and of media editors who vacillate over the disappearance of local journalism and the decimation of national newspaper, television and radio staff due to the economics of digitalisation. And we must be able to say that there is something far more important at stake—for democracy and for the capacity to speak truth to power—than the collateral damage caused by technology upgrades.

Dominating platitudes about the predicament of journalism are pitched mostly at the level of the inexorability of technological change and our relative helplessness in the face of it. Since the Industrial Revolution at least, the argument goes, this is how it has always been, and societies have always adapted and eventually benefitted from it, anyway. We should concentrate on the long-term gain that comes from any short-term pain. And there is no shortage of research that will underpin this positive view. We read it in the influential 2014 management book by Erik Brynjolfsson and Andrew McAfee titled, *The Second Machine Age: Work, Progress, and Prosperity in a Time of Brilliant Technologies*. The cheery subtitle is included because it clearly signals the authors' views on computer-based industry transformation. AI and machine learning have, they tell us, "delivered jaw-dropping results" in our time. And computer-based innovations in leading-edge activities like robotics are "enriching our world and our lives" on a near-daily basis. And more hyperbolically again, Brynjolfsson and McAfee are "convinced that [automation is] the best economic news on the planet". They *do* note the shortcomings of such disruption, and the "inflection point" that we are brought to by such rapid and comprehensive technological change. However, the best we can do is to ameliorate the very worst of these "externalities" through government intervention and investment in areas like education, skills training and the introduction of something like a universal basic income (UBI) that

DOI: 10.4324/9781003054207-2

would help those most disadvantaged by technological change. Technological change itself, however, cannot be meddled with, and neither can the capitalist "free" market that drives it.

This vaguely liberal-democratic argument might almost be uncontroversial if journalism were just another profession caught up in the endless cycles of technological transformation. It is true that as automation and AI spreads through more elite jobs like law, or accountancy and a large part of what educators or physicians do, then not many are going to miss the routine and monotonous tasks that are set to disappear. And so journalists, like everybody else, should therefore embrace change, upgrade their skill sets and modernise their craft accordingly. This mindset must be resisted. We need to be unapologetic when considering the place and role of the journalist in society. Journalism is *not* like any other profession—those regular forms of work that either evolve and thrive or become marginal or extinct due to economic or technological change. Journalism is different in at least two ways: it is *defined* by its original tools (writing and print culture) like no other profession; and it emerged during the Enlightenment as a vital element in the processes of liberal-democratic society, and as representative of the fourth estate. We can extend this by stating that journalism's 18th-century analog tools and its 18th-century political role are still the essence of what makes it function in the way that we still expect it to today: recording the facts of the world, speaking truth to power, working within a specific code of ethics, providing the communicative bloodstream of a civil society and supplying the oxygen of a public sphere. But *that* kind journalism has become frozen in time. Digital technology has transformed politics and economics, and its networks have altered forever our sense of time-space. Journalism, as a profession, has been dragged into the digital twenty-first century, but it can't do what we expect it to do because the new tools it has been forced to work with won't allow it to do what it was created to do as an 18th-century analog-based profession and craft.

The sharp dissonance between the classical theory and practice of journalism and that of digital technology is what this book seeks to explore. It is a conflict that has real-world effects that bode ill for traditional conceptions of truth, for the functioning of democracy and for the necessary configurations of civil society and the public sphere. To understand the genesis and nature of what is a *key political problem* of our time, it's necessary to frame the crisis of journalism as both a technological and a philosophical one. Technological because the broad-based transition from analog to digital signifies more than we commonly realize; and philosophical because the modernising world that journalism was born into and helped create was premised upon a culture (that of print) that the technology of writing made possible.

We begin, then, by thinking about journalism as a profession and craft that was created and defined, irreducibly, by the tools of its trade—writing and print. Before that, however, it's necessary to be clear about what is meant by the term "technology".

A word about "technology"

The philosopher Yuk Hui proposes a useful way to think about technology in his book, *The Question Concerning Technology in China*. Drawing from the so-called German School of the philosophy of technology, which includes, among others, Ernst Kapp, Martin Heidegger and Arnold Gehlen, Hui reminds us of the distinctions that are necessary when thinking conceptually about our relationship with tools. There are, in fact, three terms to consider: first is *technics*, which refers to "the general category of all forms of making and practice"; second is *techné*, which is concerned with the Greek conception of it and which Heidegger understood as equating with *poiesis*, or a "bringing forth" into being something that previously did not exist in the world; and third is the more familiar term *technology*, which designates "a radical turn which took place during European modernity, and developed in the direction of ever-increasing automation" (Hui, 2016, p. 4, note 3). The last term has a specific meaning for Heidegger that serves to give "technology" a distinctly "modern" direction of development, one that led to what he termed "Gestell", or a form of "enframing", a dominating mode of existence in the world, which, as Heidegger put it, "drives out every other possibility of revealing" (1977, p. 27).

Some precision concerning our terms of reference is necessary. Too often the word "technology" is used as shorthand for computers, and we tend to infuse that term with a sense of the innovative, the cutting-edge and the exciting. We see it in commonplace assertions like: "I would love to work in the tech industry" or the "tech stocks rallied on Wall Street today" or, in the corporate speak employed by Michael Dell of Dell Technologies, that reads: "Our business is about technology". These statements refer to computers, or computer-based processes and industries, and we generally know this. But used in this way, the term obscures more than it reveals. "Technology" is more than computers. For instance, Langdon Winner, in predigital 1980, argued that "artifacts have political qualities" and that "what matters is not technology itself, [so much as the] social or economic system in which it is embedded" (p. 122). Digitality can therefore tell us something about the "system" we live in. But what does it tell us? At an obvious level it says that the "system" today is no longer dominated by analog machines and processes. This is a point that we have collectively not thought enough about—or where we have thought about it, we tend to accept the Silicon Valley narrative that says that digital represents "progress" (see Negroponte, 1995, for a seminal perspective on this). Digital technology may represent "progress" but does so across a relatively narrow criteria—and certainly not within journalism and news media. Again, this is not a new claim (see McChesney, 2013). However, to think about the problem of digitality and journalism from the perspective of what is *an essential incompatibility* between analog and digital in terms of the communication of information is both new and illuminating.

Journalism, or more precisely, the journalist's craft, emerged and developed as an *analog* craft based on writing and print. Today, however, journalism, along with its philosophical and ethical underpinnings, still acts as though the world were still analog. But journalism is an analog profession in a hostile digital environment. It survives uneasily and is situated precariously on the verge of extinction in a new mediascape that has no necessary use for its professionalism, its moral and ethical standards, its heritage or its responsibilities as agents of the fourth estate. The traditional technology of the journalist, that of writing and the print culture it helped generate, is "technology" of the kind that once conveyed a "radical turn that took place during European modernity" but crucially, and especially in the age of computers, now it finds itself existentially susceptible to the requirements of "ever-increasing automation" as Hui phrased it (2016, p. 4). The phrases "modernity" and "ever-increasing automation" contained in Hui's definition of technology will become salient themes in this narrative. Their importance for the creation and development—*and fundamental decline*—of journalism as an analog process in the face of inexorable digitality will become clearer as the story unfolds. It argues that analog journalism cannot exist in a digital sphere. It has become diminished to the point where it operates increasingly as an ideological vector for the imperatives of corporate capital, and where the civil society and public sphere that "modern" journalism helped to create are distorted and subordinate to these same imperatives. This bleak diagnosis means that either we completely reassess the role and function of "modern" journalism, with its Enlightenment-inspired ethics and professional craft—or we reinvent it, so it functions positively (and digitally) according to the different needs of a *postmodern* technological imperative with different ethics and a different conception of what the journalistic craft of writing can contribute positively to a *digital* civil society and public sphere.

What technology reveals

One of the most famous lines written by Marx on the nature of technology first appeared as a footnote in *Capital*:

> Technology *discloses man's mode of dealing with Nature* and the process of production by which he sustains his life, and thereby also lays bare the mode of formation of *his social relations*, and of the *mental conceptions* that flow from them.
>
> (1982, p. 493, n. 4)

It's a single sentence, but it's also an extraordinarily powerful concentrate of pure political economy and analytical thought. It has three strands of insight that are italicised and will be considered in their turn. First, Marx states that *technology reveals our relationship with Nature*. And Nature, too, he observes, is itself a technology. In the same footnote, he writes with approval of Charles Darwin's *Origin of Species* as being "a history of natural technology, i.e., the formation of the organs of plants and animals which serve as the instruments of production for sustaining their life" (1982, p. 493, n.4). Reflecting his great admiration for Darwin's theory of evolution, Marx argues that humans should be seen as part of "Nature's technology" (ibid). What is explicit in this passage is that the "mode", or *form*, of technology "discloses" a great deal about thc relationship in its human-technology-Nature essentials—and that our tools say a great deal about us and our place and role in the world.

In the Western philosophical tradition this relationship has assumed an *ontological distance* whereby humans are seen as somehow separate from technology and Nature. In this view technological innovation springs from our innate problem-solving capacity and that Nature is a distinct realm there to be exploited for human needs. This is an important point and is a trope that has existed in the Western thought world since at least the time of ancient Greece. For instance, it was something that Democritus (460–370 BCE) wrote about. As Joachim Schummer writes, according to Democritus, humans imagine technological solutions by means of "imitating Nature". In other words, we took our cues from Nature, such as observing the skill of the spider in the action of "weaving and mending, or the swallow in house-building". These observations and countless others served as clues for the solution for the problems we encountered and the kinds of technologies (or *techné*) necessary to overcome them (2001, pp. 105–120). By seeing the world around us from a distance, we see it as unconnected to us. Nature appears as an alien and potentially hostile realm, something to fear or shelter from or something to manipulate and dominate through our facility for *techné*. This presumed ontological distance was echoed more influentially in the Bible, in Genesis 1:26, to be precise, which proclaims that "let Man (sic) have dominion over the fish of the sea, and over the fowl of the air, and over every living thing that moves upon the earth". By the time of early modern Europe, this idea of the apartness of humans from technology and Nature was a deeply held concept; a cultural and common-sense notion that Marx also subscribed to in his analysis of capitalism. And as Max Weber (2005) famously pointed out, capitalism itself was understood, and justifiably so in the eyes of many, to operate based upon this Old Testament idea. It's only with the emergence of the environmental consequences of the adoption of that myth that we have begun to realise how disastrous the belief has been. The idea of the human relationship with technology and Nature will be developed more fully below. It will argue that we have never stood apart from technology or from Nature; rather, we have evolved symbiotically as *analog with it*, meaning that humans *are* technology and are themselves analogical creatures.

Second, and to continue with Marx's verdict on technology and society, he tells us also about the "social relations" that sustain our "mode of dealing with Nature". These are the traditions, institutions, customs and laws that shape how people interact with other people. For Marx, industrial technology helped form specific social relations based on the "means of production". The "means", being the tools, technologies and ancillary processes, that produced the "ends", which in social terms was the formation of *a new class division*. This was between the bourgeois class, who owned the machines and factories, and the working class, who had little choice other than to sell their labour to them. Industrial technology, in other words, emerges from capitalism, which produces new divisions of social class. This idea was expressed in 1847 by Marx, albeit in a rather mechanical way, in *The Poverty of Philosophy*:

> Social relations are closely bound up with productive forces. In acquiring new productive forces men change their mode of production; and in changing their mode of production, in changing the way of earning their living, they change all their social relations. The hand-mill gives you society with the feudal lord; the steam-mill society with the industrial capitalist.

Overly deterministic or not, the point is still well made—that the advent of machines of manufacture brought about a radical change in the social relations of peoples. But there is more. Early modern theory on the economics of industrialisation, by Adam Smith and David Ricardo, and later by Marx himself, developed the concept of value-creation as a primary motive force of capitalism. The production of so-called surplus value identified a new form exploitation in the social relations generated under capital. Machines, class and the emergence of the legalised and regulated wage system not only codified the exploitation of the working class, but also compelled that class to exist as wage labour and to become dependent upon capital for their own exploitation (Marx, 1982, pp. 769, 900–902). Such a historically invidious position was very different from slave and feudal systems because waged labour was based upon the ever-ongoing development of new industrial technologies. Moreover, this position also gave rise also to the subjective phenomena of *alienation*. Here—and the concept will become important to our argument later—the worker does not own or control the means of production or the commodities they produce, but neither do they realise themselves fully as *Homo faber*, as unrestricted producers of things through their evolved technological capacities and potentials. And as Marx argued in the *Grundrisse*, instead of the tool being an extension of the hand and, with it, the mind and its intentionality, the wage-labourer in the capitalist social relation is essentially appropriated as "living labour" by the machine, which then acts upon the worker "as an alien power, as the power of the machine itself" (1973, p. 615).

The false separation from technology and from Nature is part of the social relations that are baked into capitalism. That we tend to either accept this idea, or not give much thought to it, brings us to the third of Marx's insights into the logic of technology, and that is what he called the "mental conceptions" that flow from the relationship. David Harvey, in his *The Enigma of Capital*, argues that "capital evolves" (2011, pp. 119–139). It evolves as a social relation based upon power and exploitation, and, in that evolution, it gradually shapes the "mental conceptions" of the world that reflect the narrow needs of capitalism. The mental conceptions of the world can conceivably take any form, but broadly speaking they are formulated within:

> Cultural norms and belief systems (that is, religious and political ideologies) [that] are powerfully present but do not exist independently of social relations, production and consumption possibilities and dominant technologies.
>
> (p. 122)

Reflecting the imperatives of capital creates many and changing conceptions of the world, with the enduring ones creating forms of consciousness that are not so much "false" but serve instead to obscure what Marx sought to "disclose" in the workings of capital. Stubborn conceptions may include the idea that the "free" market is positive and bureaucracy is negative; or that capitalism represents freedom and the state as unfreedom. Such conceptions also view technological change as progressive and not alienating; and as liberating opposed to exploitative. Finally, it is the widespread "mental conception" that shapes our belief that innovation in modern technology is somehow connected to actual human need and the solving of practical problems—and not reflective of the competition between capitalists to increase their share of markets and profits. However, with our mental conceptions also rooted in Greek philosophy and in Judeo-Christian ideology, the yet more ancient and deep relationship between humans as an anthropological category (*Homo sapiens*) and the technological and Natural world, remains obscured also. As a child of the Enlightenment, Marx saw humans in precisely these Greek and quasi-Judeo-Christian terms. He thought as a "modern" political economist, and notwithstanding his admiration for Darwinian evolution, he still carried the traces of premodern thinking into his analysis. And so, a major mental conception that Marx and many others have failed to consider is that we are Darwin's creatures in ways that go deeper, and with more social effects than we commonly realise. In other words, if we think more broadly, embracing anthropology as well as philosophy, then it is possible to realise that we evolved as technological beings who have never stood apart from technology or Nature. And if we consider that our ontology is analog, then this opens up new understandings of our place in the world—and it tells us more about the condition of the "modern" journalist in a "postmodern" digital mediascape.

I began with the argument that journalism faces a highly uncertain future due to the comprehensive digitalisation of not only the media industry, but also the world that journalism is a part of. The issue facing journalism is its colonisation by digital. The problem is therefore technological. Most of us understand this at some level of comprehension. However, digitalisation is far more than a disruptive technology. It is *another category* of technology, one that is driven and shaped by capitalist market forces that either incorporates or destroys the analog technologies and processes that get in its way. Journalism is presently at an impasse where it is neither fully incorporated nor destroyed. It clings tenuously to its heritage, to its ethics and (where it can) to its professional craft of writing and reporting and storytelling. But it fights a faltering rear-guard battle with the imperatives of a new category of technology that conflicts fundamentally with the print culture and time-space qualities of a profession that is essentially an 18th-century creation that cannot change without losing its 18th-century *reason for being*.

As a new category of technology, digital raises important questions about where we stand in relation to not just digital, but to the analog world that we are being dispossessed of (Hassan, 2020; 2023). In the next chapter I explore the question. This will show that we are losing rather more than we gain by placing our trust and faith in what has been essentially a gigantic social experiment, one promoted by libertarians from Silicon Valley and aided by governments that never asked their populations if a digital future is what they wanted. This faith has left the shape, speed and logic of that future to powerful neoliberal interests that have their own plans concerning the roles that these "jaw-dropping" technologies would play in all our lives.

This chapter ends by remembering what is disappearing into the virtual time-space of digital media, and by evoking what we are losing as informed political actors able to participate in discussions and debates that could make a difference. Disappearing are the forms of journalism that came into being in the secularising, revolutionising and industrialising 18th century, when, according to Eric Hobsbawm (1996), the new and radical profession of journalist "launched thunderbolts", "formulated policy", "became the voices of the poor" and were sometimes "radical demagogues" who played a vital role in the creation of a "modern world".

A historical and political sketch of the idea-typical journalist

The thumbnail history of prominent journalists that you are about to read should be understood as an ideal-typical selection taken almost, but not quite, at random. Many others could have been included. Those offered here are "ideal-typical" in Max Weber's (2012, p. 131) sense, where "the aim of [the] ideal-typical concept formation is always to bring out clearly what is *distinctive*, and *not* what is generic, in cultural formation and become of interest only in connection with another circumstance" (original emphases). In other words, the intention is to compare these short biographical sketches—and with an appropriate awareness of the myriad real-life complexities and paradoxes and inconsistencies that, with no exceptions, attend the human condition—with the logic of the torrents of writing, reporting, comment and opinion that comprises the digital journalistic profession today. The objective is to see what becomes apparent when the generic contemporary is set against the historical ideal-typical. What becomes clear in the exercise is that the journalists acting within the "ideal-typical formation" *contributed something distinctive* (though not necessarily unique) to their craft, to their profession and to society. They did so at different times in our modern history, either through their writing, through their political activities or through a combination of both. The list is far from complete or definitive, but it illustrates what modern journalism was able to achieve, and what its heritage and importance became by means of purely analog means of production and consumption.

The point of the comparison is that the world inhabited by those on the list has become technologically outmoded today. That form of modernity, in its historical distinction, and all that this distinction made possible, has passed. To be sure, many journalists today aspire to achieve distinction in their work, but they do so with tools that were invented with a different logic and for a different (or more complicated) purpose (Edwards, 1996). But a collective lack of understanding of the essential nature of digital communication means that we are unable to fully recognise that the journalism of today cannot operate effectively upon the ideals, methods and ethics of the journalism of yesterday. The analog world of modernity, of Enlightenment, of democracy, of the concept of objective truth and so on are difficult, if not impossible, for the digital journalist to effectively incorporate into their work. Nevertheless, on a formal level, the professional and ethical digital journalist of today is supposed to be guided by the same ethics as their analog forebears. The problem is that the analog journalist lived and worked in another communicative universe. And that universe is categorically incompatible with its digital descendant.

-

Thomas Paine (1737–1808), "whose weapons were the pamphlet and the pen" (van Doren, 1922), was steeped in the revolutionary fervour of early modernity. The idea of the dawning of a new age of reason was again a key motivating force for this journalist-activist. But Paine spoke truth to power in a different way than did his conservative near-contemporaries such as Edmund Burke. He was not trying to preserve an old order through his journalism but rather to create a new one, a new world inspired by the revolution in France, instead of repelled by it. Paine was the author of the acerbic anti-monarchical tract *Common Sense*. His treatise catalysed public sentiment for independence in America, selling over 100,000 copies upon publication in 1776 to an estimated two million literates in the Thirteen Colonies; and upwards of 500,000 during the seven-year struggle for American independence (Hitchens, 2008, p. 37). Paine was imbued with the Enlightenment ideas then sweeping Europe and North America by means of the revolution in print. He envisaged a new kind of human existing in a world being changed through print. Marshal McLuhan called this modern human, "typographical man" (sic), someone formed as an *individual* through reading, writing and the culture of print (1962, p. 199). In *Common Sense* Paine wrote: "We have it in our power to begin the world over again" (Paine, 2012, p. 85). And echoing McLuhan's (1962, p. 42) concept of the transformation in our "sense ratio" from hearing (in oral culture) to seeing (in print culture) by means of the technologised word, he penned what would become his famous *Letter to the Abbé Raynal* (another journalist) in Paris, in 1782, which included the words: "we see with other eyes; we hear with other ears; and think with other thoughts, than those we formerly used" (Abel, 1942, p. 183).

Paine also wrote to the *Abbé* that, "Letters are the tongue of the world" (Abel, 1942, p. 183). This is a fascinating choice of words. It's an intuitive connecting of *technology with the body* that gives rise to the intriguing thought that skilled literary craftsmen, like Paine, saw a natural resonance between pen, hand and consciousness; an analog extension that expressed a "knowing" that is the ancient, embodied and a tacit relationship, something that we are currently in the process of forgetting in our networked digitality (Sennett, 2009, p. 44). The "message" of Paine's "medium" of pamphleteering was an instance of Jürgen Habermas's public sphere in embryonic formation in North America. Richard Beeman, in his *Introduction* to a 2012 reissue of Paine's book, conjures a vivid image of its emergence, one built in no small part by the propaganda effect of *Common Sense* itself whose public reception:

> went well beyond its sales; as one Philadelphia writer observed, "it was read to all ranks"—farmers, artisans, mechanics, merchant seamen—in coffeehouses and taverns throughout America. It caused a fundamental transformation in Americans' thinking about both their relationship with their "Mother Country" and their very identity as Americans.
>
> (p. xxxii)

Habermas developed his concept to explain the significance of just the kind of modern political communication Beeman describes. In *The Structural Transformation of the Public Sphere* (1989), he brings critical social theory to the historical foundations of journalism and public debate. He also makes salient the journalists' role and function in political modernity. Habermas's work has been highly influential but has attracted criticism, too. Prominent here is Nancy Fraser, who in 1990 wrote from a feminist perspective of the narrowness of purview in Habermas's public sphere concept. For Fraser, although Habermas's theory is "indispensable to critical social theory and to democratic political practice", women and other marginalised groups were notable by their absence in it (1989, p. 57). Habermas "fails to examine other non-liberal, non-bourgeois, competing public spheres" (1989, p. 62) like working class and, most especially, women. Using historical accounts, Fraser shows that there were existing and flourishing "counterpublics"—literate and political formations in 18th-century society—that Habermas neglected to acknowledge.

These "counterpublics" are important to the journalistic narrative. They could include, in theory, almost anyone who was literate and thoughtful and read mass-media content of whatever kind, be it books, political pamphlets, science journals or the vast yellow press and entertainments media that emerged over the course of the 19th century. Such individuals and groups would constitute part of a generalised continuum of *sentiment* and *opinion* that would have been shaped and formed by the commonly recognised, if not commonly held, norms and values of the time. These would have been, as Raymond Williams writes in his *Culture and Society: 1780–1950*, and quoting the social historian R. H. Tawney, "the values, preferences, interests and ideals which rule at any moment in a given society" (1960, p. 238). And in the middle of the 19th century, these were those of a modernising and industrialising society whose extended public spheres were permeated by a spreading liberal *ethos*, albeit one tempered by the social and political stresses generated by the structural inequalities of capitalism.

This context of sentiment and opinion brings us to our next journalist, Charles Dickens (1812–1870). A novelist by fame, but also a journalist by profession, Dickens's writings had a powerful effect upon a literate and broadly Anglophone public sphere. His most celebrated works included *Oliver Twist*, which was first serialised in monthly instalments between 1837 and 1838 in the magazine *Bentley's Miscellany* (Grubb, 1941, pp. 290–291). The monthly chapters and subsequent book version became media sensations. What they helped do was draw public attention to the horrors of the workhouse system (something Dickens had personal experience of) as well as of the widespread social deprivation that scarred Victorian Britain. Mass literacy was helping to change perceptions. A limited working-class franchise was coming in Britain (in 1867), and, as Hobsbawm wrote, it then "became obvious that [the working-class] would demand—and receive—substantial public intervention for greater welfare" (1996, p. 237). Dickens's wrenching human portrayals were consumed by a public whose mental conceptions were readied for change. They helped create a climate of opinion against the exploitative excesses of industrialisation and so eased the passage of various legislative reforms during the second half of the 19th century (Boyer, 2021). By means of their tremendous popularity, Dickens's fiction and non-fiction can be seen as influential reportage, as exposure pieces of investigative journalism that pierced the consciousness and outraged the moral values of national public spheres that were informed and strengthened by a fourth estate that could educate and so construct a more sophisticated understanding of the world that could positively and functionally incorporate both Enlightenment and entertainment values.

The profession and craft of the journalist as vector for the transmission of certain liberal-democratic values and ethics does not necessarily follow a Hegelian teleology of linear historical progress. We live in a world where the modern concept of "progress" has always been spasmodic and subjectively comprehended, and one that can suffer blockage or reversal at any time (Gray, 2003). The corrupted and the compromised, the career-obsessed and the anti-democratic, the cynical and the opportunistic have always peopled the ranks of the fourth estate. But they are not the focus here. The "ideal-typical" journalist is. Moreover, that "ideal-typical concept formation" contains countervailing tendencies, an *alter ego* that "becomes of interest", as Weber put it, such that it can serve to sharpen our view of the more *positive distinctiveness* of the journalists portrayed in these vignettes. A case in point is the work of Walter Lippmann (1889–1974), an American journalist and critic. In 1922, the same year as James Joyce's high-modernist *Ulysses* was printed in Paris, Lippmann's *Public Opinion* was published. It was a seminal moment in critical media studies. The book was essentially a critique of the principles upon which journalism was founded. In the mass-media age, Lippmann argued, it is *information*, not truth, that is the central media resource. For him, truth, objectivity and professional ethics become the inevitable casualties of the formation of a mass-media news industry. Functioning as an industry, and with the necessary hierarchical structures of production oriented primarily towards the selling of newspapers, means that the product of journalism is something easily "manufactured" and so provides "opportunities for manipulation … to anyone who understands the process" (2012, p. 135).

The "manufacture of consent" was an idea taken up more recently by Noam Chomsky, who argued similarly that mass-media systems are essentially "powerful ideological institutions that carry out a system-supportive propaganda function, by reliance on market forces, internalised assumptions, and self-censorship, and without overt coercion" (Herman & Chomsky, 1988, p. 306). This is now a mainstream perspective in critical media studies, although with the emergence of social media and the Internet, the role and function of "powerful ideological institutions" is now a more complex phenomenon. The logic of the claim still has validity, however, and will be discussed later in the context of digitality. The point here, however, is to look at Lippmann's critique of journalism as it was at the time, in the early part of the 20th century. A defence against Lippmann's attack was mounted early on by the philosopher and educational reformer John Dewey (1859–1952) in his *The Public and Its Problems*, published in 1927. Dewey saw merit in Lippmann's hypothesis, but he thought it went too far, was too negative in its suggestion that the public was simply a passive herd that, through the manipulation and manufacture of news, could be persuaded not so much about what to think, but what to think about. Dewey countered this negativity by pointing out that there was still hope and possibility within mass-media structures. A public and democracy could come together within a media sphere, he maintained, but it would require a responsibility of people to *engage more* as citizens, as readers, writers, journalists and audiences, and to communicate, openly and freely and without either the suppressing or censoring of others. Without such a literate and engaged public, democracy is impossible, he claimed. By applying these basic principles to new technological contexts, Dewey wrote, mass media could be made more democratic through accessible and active citizen communication:

> Our modern state-unity is due to the consequences of technology employed to facilitate the rapid and easy circulation of opinions and information … so as to generate constant and intricate interaction far beyond the limits of face-to-face communities.
>
> (2012, p. 103)

Thus, through modern media technologies, a way must be found so that the public can once again "recognize and articulate itself" (2012, p. 108). For Dewey, the key was to overcome the "technopoly" (Postman, 1992)—i.e., the dominance of the logic of capitalist technology over civil society—and the resultant political apathy that was frustrating genuine democratic engagement. Success in this could transform what he called the "Great Society", one created by the 19th-century machine age, into the "Great Community" of the more technologically advanced 20th century (2012, p. 110). "Communication can alone create a great community", Dewey wrote, but until the control of the means of communication is democratised, then "the Public will remain in eclipse" (2012, p. 118). Dewey gives us a diagnosis but not a prognosis for what remains a difficult issue. But what he also provides across the full scope of his book is an example of the distinguishing mark of an Enlightenment-based *autocritique*. That is to say, the expression of the intellectual capacity (in Lippmann as well as Dewey) to look objectively and critically at the processes of the powerful media institutions, as well as the journalists' part in their functioning. Moreover, Lippmann and Dewey offer a healthy scepticism towards journalists' truth-claims and the technological and technocratic systems that enable them. They provide too a moral-ethical compass, an orientation to the ways and means of staying true, whether explicitly articulated or not, to the culture of scepticism that must be intrinsic to public communication.

Our two final "ideal-typical" journalists constitute a leap over several decades to nearer our own time. Both are women, and therefore they constitute an essential element of Fraser's "counterpublics" who took what was their due as moderns who just happened to be female. Marie Colvin (1956–2012) and

Anna Politkovskaya (1958–2006), an American and a Russian, war and investigative correspondents, were writers who were embodiments of a certain kind of journalism. They were a part of the craft where words are more important, and have more real-life human consequences, than perhaps in any other. War and investigative reporting deal with subjects and forces that for most of us remain mental abstractions; death by violence, suffering, displacement, loss, a world completely turned on its head. Colvin and Politkovskaya went to where the worst of human capacities for inhumanity occurred and reported it. Their words contained the potential for some large or small insights into what they witnessed. Their words were the basis of a form of understanding, and perhaps to something eventually being put right or atoned for—and with the public sphere being an incrementally better place because of our engagement with their words.

Marie Colvin was in many ways the classical Western foreign correspondent, following a path taken mostly by men since the First World War when conflict began to take on a more global and interconnected significance. The loss of an eye in 2001 to grenade shrapnel in the Sri Lankan civil war (1983–2009) speaks to the kind of engagement with the subject, albeit tragic, that Dewey saw as integral to the point and to the value of public communication. In 2010, two years before she was killed in Syria, Colvin gave a speech on the importance of war journalism, and she emphasised the function and interrelation between media technology and the physical body of the journalist:

> In an age of 24/7 rolling news, blogs and Twitters, we are on constant call wherever we are. But war reporting is still essentially the same—*someone has to go there and see what is happening*. You can't get that information without going to places where people are being shot at, and others are shooting at you. The real difficulty is having enough faith in humanity to believe that enough people be they government, military or the man on the street, will care when your file reaches the printed page, the website or the TV screen. We do have that faith because we believe we do make a difference.
>
> (Colvin, 2010) (emphasis added)

Anna Politkovskaya is similar but different. A Russian who reported on the crimes of the Russian state in what she termed Russia's wars of "imperial ambition" (Politkovskaya, 2003, p. 205) in Chechnya between 1994 and 2005. She was like Marie Colvin in that they both worked in spheres of physical danger. They differed in that Politkovskaya focussed mainly on the investigative side of speaking truth to power as opposed to revealing the physical horrors of war by being there and writing about it. This is not to say that Politkovskaya did not visit war zones. She did, often, and indeed her assassination, a crime the Russian authorities never seriously investigated, was, in the view of many of her colleagues and other observers, a direct result of her reporting on visits to Chechnya for the Moscow-based magazine *Novaya Gazeta.* There she uncovered multiple war crimes committed by the Russian regime and by the henchmen of its local client, the Kadyrov warlord family (see Gall & De Waal, 1997, pp. 228–255). Politkovskaya differed too in that she lived and worked in a country hostile to the journalism of free inquiry. A public sphere had emerged cautiously after the collapse of the USSR in 1992, and much that was previously taboo was now being written about and read. Indeed, as Georgi Derluguian wrote in his 'Introduction' to Politkovskaya's book, *A Small Corner of Hell*: *Dispatches from Chechnya*, "After the loosening of press controls in 1986, the circulation of the most daring publications soared to stratospheric heights and their journalists became public heroes" (2003, p. 6). Press freedom had no history in Russia and so the new blossoming was always liable to suppression. Politkovskaya wrote on the point of her work and the importance of its continuation as the window of press freedom in Russia began to close in the late 1990s:

> It is necessary to mention that Russian society was overwhelmingly opposed to the [Chechen] war, not to a small degree because Russian journalists in their last moment of professional glory exposed, with great passion, the war's senselessness and ghastly reality.
>
> (2003, p. 20)

Colvin and Politkovskaya, like most journalists, had no formal power but possessed a "professional glory", an authenticity that was expressed in their immutable words. Politkovskaya was modest in that she claimed not to be a "war correspondent" but rather "just a civilian [which] gives me that much deeper an understanding of other civilians, living in Chechen towns and villages, who are caught in the war" (2003, p. 26). Humility aside, only words written by someone who went there to see what was happening could convey her "understanding" and perhaps an empathy in the minds of her readers, who in Russia, as in much of the rest of the world, read and wrote in what were the dying days of more than two centuries of print culture and the inspirational forms public understanding it could produce.

As an "ideal-typical" list, our journalists embody the "distinctive" character of journalistic work that becomes of social, political and technological "interest", as Weber put it "in connection with another circumstance". We have that other circumstance today. One communicative universe is fast disappearing, and another emerges by means of the commercially conceived and corporately imposed digitalisation of journalism. Digitalisation has been called a "revolution" since its mass inception during the 1980s. Tech entrepreneurs sold it then, as they later sold mobile phones, as the means of a business revolution. Bill Gates titled the first chapter of his 1996 book *The Road Ahead,* 'The Revolution Begins'. But it was more than a revolution in business. Writing in the same year as Gates, technology theorists Mark Weiser and John Seely Brown predicted a more widely spread revolution, an age of "ubiquitous computing" where machines become "so imbedded, so fitting, so natural, that we use [them] without even thinking about it" (1996). No one was asking for them then or demanded them later. Computerisation happened *to* us. And itwas mostly imposed, at work, in leisure and in the culture more widely as digitalisation began to permeate increasing registers of life, especially after the emergence of Web 2.0 around 2004.

So, this is a proper revolution. However, it does not "devour its children" as Tom Paine's conservative journalist contemporary Jacques Mallet du Pan supposed all revolutions do (Kennedy, 2002, p. 113). But this is first and foremost a technological revolution, not a social one. Society is "revolutionised" only as an after effect. Being a capitalist revolution primarily means that it is logical and rational—and inhuman. It operates at the level of machines and networked systems that rationalise society in a particular way towards particular ends. It is a revolution that *creates* its children in the form of users; but it "devours" its technological antecedents and the kind of world they made possible. In the case of journalism—based on analog writing tools, print-based culture and human-scaled communication forms and processes, the 1986 Wapping Dispute and the eclipse of old Fleet Street[1] was a portent of the death of one form of journalism and the creation of a new kind. Journalism's decline as a craft and profession with its ancient tools and ethics, however, was relatively slow within the wider social revolution brought on by ubiquitous computing. Web 2.0 and the social media explosion helped to hurry along this process of decline. X and Facebook, for example, helped to disconnect journalists from their analog tools and compel them to spend more time with digital screens and smartphones. This "upgrading" signified a loss of the tacit knowledge of craft journalism, of the feel for the beat and its people and processes, and the capacity (and time) for reflection to make sense of the work within the context of an ethical code.

The veteran British journalist Neal Ascherson was interviewed in the *Observer* on the occasion of his 90th birthday, and he noted, balefully and sympathetically, with his younger colleagues in mind, that "Journalism was easier in my time, you had more time to think" (Ascherson, 2022). Ascherson was speaking of the time required to do a difficult job, to obtain information, to check its veracity, corroborate, discuss, draft, revise, etc. This was never an open-ended timeframe, but journalistic craft skills, training, contacts, knowledge of the subject and the act writing itself made a difficult job of communication easier and faster. Journalism today has never been easier or faster. But that is now the problem. Such "efficiency" is now achieved by computerisation, algorithmic logic and the deskilling of any part of the process that may be made subjected to automation.

It's not possible to know exactly where this process will end up ten or fifteen years from now. What is certain is the computational power that transformed journalism and the media is only going to become more powerful. Subsequent chapters will show how far this process has come already, with the unleashing onto an unsuspecting world, by Microsoft, Google, OpenAI and others, of proprietary versions of AI software based upon powerful algorithms that can more or less plausibly mimic journalistic texts "written" by every one of our "ideal types". But our analysis would be only surface description without a deeper philosophical perspective to enable us to understand the roots of the problem. If the perspective is properly oriented towards questioning the aspects of the problem that matter most, such as a critical appraisal of the singular role of journalism in democratic societies, then a more philosophical-anthropological inquiry into the human relationship with the analog tools and technologies of writing upon which journalism was formed is necessary. We need to understand the place of the journalist in a particular kind of technological society, a society that is both capitalist and digital. And we must develop a critical consideration of the deep contradiction that all journalists face: being ethically committed to an 18th-century profession of the reporting of "truth" through printed words in the form of narrativised stories that are becoming all but impossible to produce and consume in the same way through digital means.

We now consider the foundations of a theory of analog and the human relation with technology (Hassan, 2023). We develop the proposition that we are analog people from an analog past, a past that has a deep and distant prehistory, a history before writing, but a history and a relationship to technology that would eventually produce writing, and this writing would make possible the whole civilisational and modern world as it existed right up until the latter part of the 20th century. That change is so very recent and has come so very fast—and the digital revolution devours its analog antecedents in journalism, in the media and in the wider economy, culture and society every hour of every day.

Note

1 Rupert Murdoch's News International went on strike to protest the computerisation of the company's editorial and printing operations in a purpose-built facility in Wapping, about three miles away from the old Fleet Street buildings in central London. The defeat of the strikers after a 54-week holdout was a symbolic moment but also the beginning of the end for the craft of journalism. On the surface, the defeat meant the obsolescence of a particular aspect of newspaper production: the Linotype production method that had brought the journalist's words, via the typesetter, to the mass-media market for over a hundred years. Historically and culturally, it meant the start of the practical attenuation of the analog process of writing and reading, and what this accomplished in the forging of a public sphere, a process going back to the beginnings of journalism in the early modern period. For the entirety of that era, from early modernity until 1986, the technological extensions that were the industrialisation of writing and reading, of pen and paper, proved to be immensely powerful tools.

2 What is analog, and why does it matter anymore?

Words matter

For the journalist, words are important. Precision and clarity are more than a "desirable" part of the job description. However, and to cite from George Orwell's essay, *Politics and the English Language*: "Many [words] are used without knowledge of their meaning" (2021, p. 17). It is not evident that things are better today than in Orwell's time. Moreover—and Orwell would agree—some words are more important than others. For instance, political words like "woke" have had their original meaning captured by powerful conservative, institutional and media interests and are used against their original constituency as a form of abuse and are "used mockingly [to describe an] over righteous liberalism" (Poole, 2019). And just as consequentially for the arguments here, commonplace words like "progress" and "efficiency" are words that, unlike "woke", have been *depoliticised* and rendered uncontroversial and apparently self-evident, and so to be deployed routinely with meanings that have become impoverished.

A similar crisis of meaning has attended the word *analog* for some time—a word, as we shall see, that's measurably disappearing from our vocabulary. This is more than a cause for minor regret. It's vitally important because where "analog" is still used, the meaning is almost always narrowly defined and therefore diminished in its potential illumination. When writing we easily adopt the habit of habit. This is the case with a word like analog, whose meaning on the surface seems clear. We use it in a sense that we imagine reflects its meaning. But when we use it in speech, publish it in print or online, we obscure it further with our restricted definition. One could object at this point that what does it matter if the word is *vanishing* from our discourses? We've all moved on. Analog *is* history. The analog processes of writing and printing have been eclipsed by pixel-generated words that radiate from millions of screens. This is "efficiency". Digitality has created *mutability* instead of *fixity* in writing. With handwriting and typing replaced by "word processing", words can be composed, deleted, rewritten, redeleted, written again, then shared instantly with a single individual or with millions through a network. Supposedly, this was not only time "efficient" but was "progress" too since

DOI: 10.4324/9781003054207-3

the network's horizontality is potentially inclusive and therefore potentially democratic.

However, the meanings of consequential terms like "efficiency" and "progress" form part of the constrained and constraining vocabulary that make up our "mental conceptions", which, as Marx reminded us, flow from the dominant social relations that give contemporaneous society their defining characteristics. "Efficiency" and "progress" are especially damaging in this respect. The acceleration of everyday life though digitality means that as producers and consumers we increasingly tend to skim over the surface of words and meaning. This is a coping strategy to deal with information overload and the "poverty of attention" that acceleration engenders in our media relationships (Hassan, 2012, p. 111). In this sense, efficiency with words does not result in profundity or reflexiveness with words, but rather more a superficiality, and a level of disconnect from meaning and etymology. This cannot be said to be progress.

Back to our concern with analog. "Efficiency" and "progress" are the words written on its tombstone, and with "digital" named as its inheritor. It is something of an irony that analog's decline is captured in their historical traces through data generated by Google. Its programme Ngram collects data from a two-decades long project of digitising—indiscriminately—as many and as various of the world's books as possible. Google scanned over 40 million volumes over the life of the 2004–2019 project. A feature of Ngram is that you can key in a word, and it will search its databases for the frequency of that word in books dating from the 1500s until 2019. "Analog" first appeared in English-language books around the early 1800s. The Ngram graph-line for "analog" hardly registers on the chart and it flat lines from 1800 until the mid-1940s. However, at the 1947 point the graph line spikes upwards until reaching its high point in the mid-1980s, whereupon it plunges as steeply as it rose. This trajectory becomes interesting when compared with a similar search conducted for "digital". "Digital" makes its registerable appearance around the same time as "analog", in the 1940s, and its line parallels that of "analog" nearly exactly. Their graph lines travel in unison until the mid-1980s, when "analog" begins its steep downward curve, and "digital" continues to soar upwards until the 2019 end of the scanning process. What's going on?

The decline of a word tells us something. It signals the loss of a concept, which is then also a loss of the diversity of understandings that has shaped human cultures for millennia. It indicates too a depletion in our cognitive store of meanings through which the world makes sense to us. What the Ngram comparison shows is that analog as a concept and as a meaningful word was, through the printed literature, essentially defined by its relationship with digital. It became understood as the antithesis of digital. Whereas digital came to be seen as a term for efficiency and progress, analog came to stand for, if not fully its opposite, then at least something obsolete and technically surpassed. Nicholas Negroponte, the early digital technology booster, reminded us of this in his 1995 book *Being Digital*, when he wrote that analog was now seriously "old-fashioned", and that analog-based media companies were in danger of becoming "old-age homes for analog thought" (pp. 38–39).

Emerging as the new way to organise computing machines in the 1940s, digital roused the meaning of analog out of its long stagnation to become *redefined* by it. Digital rose to frequency use and defined analog in relation to itself, causing analog to be understood almost *exclusively as a technology*, and as a form and logic that has or would be superseded. This is an important part of the understanding of analog and will come into my arguments a little later. But for now, let me preface those by sharing a widely held definition—in the science and technology community anyway—of the different forms and logics of both analog and digital. As part of the celebrated New York Macy Conferences of the 1940s and 1950s, the neurophysiologist and behavioural scientist R. W. Gerard was a discussant at the March 1950 session that was titled "Some of the Problems Concerning Digital Notions in the Central Nervous System". He said: "In the analogical system there are continuity relations; in the digital, discontinuity relations" (Gerard, 1953, p. 172). Continuity and discontinuity—this was an important distinction, and the wider sense of Gerard's contribution does not focus exclusively on computers but on the human nervous system. However, this high-level conference was dominated by world-renowned physicists and computer scientists like John von Neumann and Norbert Wiener. What this meant was that the connotations of these two words—would their "continuous"- "discontinuous" logics—solidify into a narrow technological sense, in the minds of both the research establishments and, more latterly, in the public mind as well (de Vaujany and Mitev, 2017, pp. 379–407).

The era in which this reclassification took place is significant. Digital computing emerged after the Second World War as a key Cold War technology. It came to be recognised by military engineers and scientists in the United States especially as a faster and more efficient means of computation in vital command and control systems. From the 1950s through to the 1970s, digital computing began to dominate over analog computing in what Paul N. Edwards (1996, pp. 71–73) called a "closed world" of "technocratic discourse" within the context of enormous government contracts in top secret projects and through covert military applications. The discontinuous logic of digital computing had another consequential application. It constituted the basis of the data protocols that made the Internet possible through the ARPANET project that began in 1969. Around this time the word "digital" increased massively in the Google Ngram frequency count and "analog" began its plummet into fixity of meaning and relative obscurity as an outmoded technological form. Analog's fate is reflected in the networked information systems that govern much of our lives today. For example, a Google image search for "analog" delivers monotonous images of mostly analog signals (continuous waves), analog clocks and analog meters with the needle that sweeps across a continuity of numbers from zero to a defined limit. A Wikipedia search defaults to the same "analog signal" definition. And because it scrapes this Internet for its information OpenAI's GPT gives almost an identical answer. In answer to the question "What is analog?", GPT replied:

> The term "analog" typically refers to a type of signal or device that represents information using continuous physical quantities. In contrast to digital signals or devices, which represent information using discrete values, analog signals or devices use continuously varying signals to convey information.

A book project I developed over 2020–2023 aimed to rediscover more varied definitions of "analog" and what this suggests about our relationship with technology, and I direct the reader to it (Hassan, 2023). Briefly, the book excavates the etymology of "analog" and builds a wider and more inclusive definition that leads to the argument, which I will sketch in outline, that humans *evolved* as technology, or *technics*—and that this reached a phase or creative peak, with the rise of Yuk Hui's "modernity" (2016, p. 4). This modernity produced the craft of the journalist, and the journalist, in turn, helped create modernity. It was the fragmentation of that modernity, of the "grand narratives"—the stories and knowledge and facts and truths that an analogically bound historical community of journalists and philosophers and writers of all kinds produced to make sense of the modern world—that inaugurated our present postmodernity. And as Jean-François Lyotard (1979, pp. 1–9) argued in his prophetic *The Postmodern Condition: A Report on Knowledge*, computing was at the very heart of the transformation. So, with this in mind, let us consider further the fragmentation of modernity and the concurrent rise of computation, and what this means for the traditional journalist and their relationship with words produced and consumed though analog means.

Digitality as historical inflection point

Samuel Johnson (1709–1784) was not a journalist, but he was an extraordinary wordsmith who understood those whose relationship with the tools of the trade he shared. In his essay "Of the Duty of the Journalist" he saw journalists in equable terms and with a critical eye: at once not only ethically lazy and often deceptive, but also as people who are unique in society, as legitimate "regulators of opinion", and more uniquely still as:

> above most other men, [those who] ought to be acquainted with the lower orders of mankind, that he may be able to judge, what will be plain, and what will be obscure; what will require a Comment, and what will be apprehended without Explanation. He is to consider himself not as writing

> to Students or Statesmen alone, but to Women, Shopkeepers, and Artisans, who have little time to bestow upon mental attainments, but desire, upon easy terms, to know how the world goes; who rises, and who falls; who triumphs, and who is defeated.
>
> (Johnson, 1758)

The finer detail of Johnson's opinion is instructive as it illuminates journalism through the eyes of an observant contemporary. It is also an example of the granularity of scale that he took to his most famous work, the 1775 *Dictionary of the English Language*. He gives "analog" similarly detailed treatment and offers the general sense of the word as it was understood in early modernity. The first edition is available online and contains several related entries to analog, the important one being "analogical", which, Johnson notes, is derived from "analogy". "Analogical" is closer to our own requirements and is defined straightforwardly as "having the quality of representing relation", as is "analogous", defined as: "having resemblance or relation". Nowhere in all the connected entries is there any reference either to technology or to people, but to "having relations" which means, logically, it could mean both.

Johnson's *Dictionary* became the model for the genre. The *Oxford English Dictionary* (OED) began to compile its own in 1857 and was more focused with the entry on "analog" and gives a definition that remains in its pages today: "A thing which (or occasionally person, who) is analogous to another; a parallel, an equivalent". A thing or a person. People are mentioned in the earliest entries on analog. You wouldn't know it today. This is because the characteristic of personhood was erased when "digital" plucked it from the low-frequency use obscurity it had been in since 1800. And analog would have been a low-frequency word forever if it had not been for the Cold War–driven imperatives of digital computing. Digitality reframed what Jonathan Sterne (2016, p. 32) called the "general senses" of analog into a narrow opposite of itself; a singularly technological form whose logic is still defined as "continuous" but whose days are all but ended—eclipsed by the "discontinuous" logic of digital computing and the new world it brought into being.

The speed of the eclipse was such that questions based upon more philosophical concerns did not feature much in the information revolution. Beginning in the late 1970s, initially in the Anglosphere, the political choices that would bring globalisation, the neoliberalisation and financialisaton of their economies and societies, ran synchronously with the emergence of widespread computerisation. The consequences of such neglect cannot be underestimated. Isolated voices in the academy warned of the dangers of experimental technologies being foisted upon societies by corporations that took little or no account of the consequences (e.g., Lyotard, 1979; Virilio, 1995; Wilder, 1997; Edwards, 1996). However, such voices declined by the end of the 1990s to be replaced by a more passive acceptance of the "inevitable" march of progress or by a retreat into endless theorising about this or that sub-category of digitalisation. And functioning at the ideological level, a widespread boosterism, promoted by the very media it enthusiastically embraced, i.e., a burgeoning Internet, served to enchant the public rather more than inform it (e.g., Gates, 1996; Rheingold, 2000; Brynjolfsson and McAfee, 2014).

The fundamental questions still need to be asked, however. A problem is that where humans stand in relation to both analog and digital technologies is the question that almost no one thought to ask. Until digital arrived, analog dominated technology use, and so the question: "where do we stand?" could not logically suggest itself. To approach the question today, we need to be guided by our philosophical inheritance. The issue of human-technology relations runs deep in Western thought. However, classical Greece also could not pose the "where do we stand?" question and so viewed technology from an ontologically narrow perspective—one that has influenced centuries of thought on the matter. As we saw earlier, by applying reason and logic as he understood it, Democritus implied a *separation* of humans from nature and technology. Aristotle, too, thought that "technology imitates nature", suggesting an ontological divide between humans, technology, and the material world (Schummer, 2001, pp. 3–4). The notion of separation has therefore had a long historiographic legacy and is present in the works of major Western philosophers like Isaac Newton, Rene Descartes and Martin Heidegger. We see it also in more contemporaneous technology thinking that develop various articulations of cybogism, or the integration of the body and the machine, and we see this in Donna Haraway's *Cyborg Manifesto* (1985), and Katherine N. Hayles' *How We Became Posthuman* (1999). This new world forces us to think more creatively

A fish doesn't know it's in water

Despite our philosophical limitations, dissatisfaction with idea of the supposedly non-overlapping realms of human life and technology has nonetheless prompted various attempts to build a more holistic perspective. For example, philosophical anthropology seeks a better grasp of our technological present by examining our prehistorical past. A major scholar in this regard is Arnold Gehlen who claims that there is no clear division between humans and technology. In his book *Man in the Age of Technology*, Gehlen writes that in our present evolutionary state, a physical and cognitive state that stretches back 200,000 years, we are born "unfinished"—deficient creatures who are "poorly equipped with sensory apparatus, naturally defenceless, naked, constitutionally embryonic through and through [and] possessing only inadequate instincts" (1980, p. 4). For Gehlen, it was an *evolutionary drift toward technology use* that formed the successful relationship between "man and his organic and instinctual deficiencies" within a potentially hostile natural environment.

In other words, we evolved into living and thinking technological forms, enabling us to survive (and thrive) *as* technological creatures.

Our elemental unity with technology *as* technological beings occurred hundreds of thousands of years ago. It was expressed as an evolutionary struggle for life, where countless mutations and adaptations in our biology over numberless generations led to a point when our species' capacity as toolmakers and users reached a level where humans could finally maintain life in a sustainable and durable way. This connection finds physical and cognitive manifestation in what Gehlen calls the "circle of action", an ancient dialectical process where:

> the analogous process of the external world bespeaks a "resonance" which conveys to man an intimate feeling for his very nature, by focusing on what echoes his nature in the external world. And if we today still speak of the "course" of the stars and of the "running of machines", the similarities thus evoked are not in the least superficial; they convey to men certain distinctive conceptions of their own essential traits based on 'resonance'. Through these similarities man interprets the world after his own image, and vice-versa, himself after his image of the world.
>
> (p. 14)

Gehlen uses the word "analogous" at the beginning of the quote but concentrates more on what he sees as a "resonance" to describe the connection that forms the "circle of action". The word is from the Latin *resonantia*, which means an "echo" or "reverberation". It also brings to mind a kind of subjective "feeling", something tacit and embodied. But this is useful only up to a point. It is the "circle of action" metaphor, standing over his entire conceptual framework, that provides the more imaginative conceptual move. It is an idea that emerged later in Marshall McLuhan who emphasises more strongly the sense of co-constitution that I want to develop further.

A fundamental axiom that's often attributed to McLuhan's 1964 *Understanding Media* reads, "we shape our tools and afterwards our tools shape us" (e.g., Naughton, 2011). It's a decent line, and although McLuhan would have agreed with it, he did not say it. The sense of McLuhan's argument was written by a reviewer of McLuhan's book, by one John Culkin, who wrote in *The Saturday Review* in 1967: "We become what we behold … we shape our tools and afterwards our tools shape us" (p. 54). Nonetheless, in his co-constitutive view, McLuhan takes the connection between humans and technology a step closer towards a singular, material and "continuous" dialectic than Gehlen was prepared to take. But neither were able to make the final conceptual move to saying that *humans are themselves technology*, and *that technology is analog*. They could not make that move because their worlds were wholly analog; and they, like all of humankind prior to the digital ascendancy, did not have the technological comparison point that would prompt a fundamentally different theoretical approach (Hassan, 2023).

Although it is an element of his language theory that's mostly overlooked, Noam Chomsky's early works on linguistic anthropology provides conceptual support to the analog theory. Language, we easily forget, is a technology, a cognitive one. And the "cognitive revolution" of about 70,000 years ago was prompted by changes in our evolutionary biology, making our species "more and more exceptional" (Harari, 2014, p. 170) in respect to the human-technology relationship. Chomsky argues that the capacity for language is part of our "genetic endowment" (1978), a heritable trait, and a capacity that we acquired in our evolution as tool users. It could be conjectured, indeed, that it was the evolved capacity for toolmaking that made us technological beings and was the capacity that matured sufficiently through genetic mutation during our ancient prehistory that lay the ground for the revolution in cognition and the emergence of language (Chomsky, 1993, p. 30). This transformation in our species was precursor to the Agricultural and later Scientific Revolution that were expressions of our cognitive capacities functioning as increasingly complex human-analog technologies emerging from an evolved and increasingly complex agency. Writing and print would act as a launch pad for the Scientific Revolution and would create a new world wherein journalism was possible and could flourish.

The medium is the message: analog words in print

Words matter more than just meaning. Words matter more than we know—written words, especially. When alphabetic script first emerged around 4,000 years ago, the mutual co-constitution process played upon the individual in an exceptionally transformative way. Working upon the oral form of consciousness that existed in prehistoric times, the practice of writing altered radically what it meant to be human in the world. Writing facilitated a new form of communication, but it also changed the ways in which we think *as* humans; indeed, the changes have been claimed to be neurophysiological in that the very organisation of brain function was altered, creating a "reading brain" (see Wolf, 2007). Walter Ong, in his essay "Writing is a technology that restructures thought" (1992), argued that with the development of writing and literacy, the technology of the written mark "takes possession of consciousness" (p. 293). Writing thus appears as endowed with almost supernatural powers in that "it tends to arrogate to itself supreme power by taking itself as normative for human expression and thought" (ibid).

Through written words, writers and readers developed self-consciousness, where the words expressing thought were transferred from the mind to the page and from the page to the mind. In other words, writing exteriorised, spatialised and temporalised words for people who began to see themselves as separate from them (see Jaynes, 1976, p. 246). In oral cultures, the word, and so the idea, the story, the referent, had existence only in sound; it was embodied in both hearing and speaking. It was evanescent. In typographic cultures, words "are not mere exterior aids, but also interior transformations of consciousness" (Ong, 1980, pp. 71–81). And so, the idea, the story, the referent was something fixed in time-space upon the printed page, awaiting its "silent scanning" by a reading public (Eisenstein, 1979, p. 93). Self-consciousness was in tension with a world "out there", a public world of abstracted expression and thought. And as literacy grew, so did the public world and the quantity of printed information in the books, pamphlets, journals and newspapers that sustained it.

The independent discourse that writing promoted contained another "supreme power". Ong again:

> Like the oracle or the prophet, the [book] relays an utterance from a source, the one who really "said" or wrote the book. The author might be challenged if only he or she could be reached, but the author cannot be reached in any book. There is no way to directly refute a text. [...] This is one reason why "the book says" is popularly tantamount to "it is true".
>
> (1982, p. 77)

"It is written", says the Bible, suggesting that which is written (in the Bible) is true. To some extent, this vatic quality attached itself to most forms of printed words and to serious journalism, too. What gave the printed word the appearance of truth is that the words themselves are given the power of authenticity by the indisputable fact of their being upon a page. This is the power of "closure" for Ong. Printed words, especially in cultures where literacy was thinly spread and a privilege, contained the "aura" of authority, presenting to the reader as something true and "uninvolved with all else ... somehow self-contained, complete" (1982, p. 129). Being "complete" meant there was nothing else to be said. It is written, and so seemingly objective, existing in splendid isolation, and therefore, authoritative and true.

If writing transformed the cognitive processes of the individual human, then the invention of typography transformed the material world. And as Elizabeth Eisenstein noted in an essay on the purpose of her 1979 book, *The Printing Press as Agent of Change*: "although everyone seemed to agree that the consequences of the advent of printing were of great importance, they all stopped short of telling us just what those consequences were" (2002, p. 87). Something similar about a "stopping short" could be said about journalism in the era of what Eisenstein called "print culture" (1979, pp. 1–92). The "consequences" of journalism and of its role as a technology-dependent agent are usually discussed as being essentially in the same category as commercial newspapers. However, the analog technology of newspaper printing was different from that of the journalist. The newspaper business was a capitalist business that always sought to become more technologically "efficient" and competitive. It finally transcended its analog roots in its transition to digital, beginning symbolically with the Wapping dispute in 1986. It is significant, if not surprising, that the defeat of the old printing unions at Wapping produced consternation for journalists everywhere (Littleton, 1992). Nonetheless, we can discern much regarding the consequences for journalism by looking at the historical trajectory of newspapers, functioning as the principal disseminators of the journalist's craft in its defining phase during the Enlightenment when analog print (and its print culture) was cutting edge communication.

The Age of Enlightenment was also an age of revolution, one that activist elements of journalism helped stoke and could be further radicalised by in turn. Robert Darnton argues that the "guild publishing" of the pre-1789 type, where the monopolies that had set the standards of the craft and protected the interests of their members, came under attack from what he called "revolutionary journalism". This was evident not only in France, but also across Europe and North America (1979, p. 503). Darnton writes that the "casual, epistolary style" of guild journalism, with its "offhand views" and where "advertisements could hardly be distinguished from news" was existentially challenged by the new writing formed within this politically febrile atmosphere (p. 260). For the new radical journalism, where in France, for example "two hundred and fifty newspapers burst into print during the last six months of 1789" (p. 482), the ideas of equality, reason, democracy, etc. not only infused the explosion of political journalism, but also brought to the fore the physical person of the journalist as an influential figure in the struggles over political ideas. Eisenstein's research on the print culture of the time notes the parallel emergence of the "Republic of Letters", defined as a "commonwealth of learning that transcended distance through access to and exchange of information" (1979, p. 168). This was an informal exchange of correspondence between prominent *philosophes* of the time. And the ideas of contemporary political theory, emanating often from journalists like Diderot, Marat, Voltaire, Paine, Franklin and Cobbett, was where ideas were refined or discarded but, above all, circulated through a private network to be later articulated in a public sphere.

The "Republic of Letters" was an 18th-century analog form of time-space compression, a shrinking of the world though the circulation of print. This constituted the major innovative "message" of the analog medium. For perhaps the first time in history, the world could be thought of as something like a singular social entity, even if the thought was illusory. It was an earlier instance of what Roland Robertson, writing about the globalisation of the early 1990s, termed "a compression of the world and the intensification of consciousness of the world as a whole" (1992, p. 8). This is an important point, one that points to a specifically analog character of the journalism of the time, one based upon not only the technologies of the time, but also the humans who worked with and through them. In the co-constitution process, the physical and cognitive capacities of the human writer and reader were both limited by and expanded by the tools of Gutenberg-enabled print culture. This is primarily an issue of scale. Benedict Anderson, in his 1983 *Imagined Communities,* wrote about these limitations and expansions. He used the epithet "print capitalism" instead of print culture, emphasising that, for him, capitalism was the motive force for the spread of print, whereas for Eisenstein "print culture" was nomenclature for its sociological expression.

Analog in space-time

Silvia Estévez is an anthropologist who researches diasporas and their digital communication practices and tells us something about how scale functions generally in the context of analog humans. She published a fieldwork essay titled "Is Nostalgia Becoming Digital?" that looks at the mobile phone use of Ecuadorian migrants. First, she states flatly that humans are analog (2009, p. 402) and proceeds to give some splendid insights that relate to the "continuity relations" that are the classical distinguishing marker of Gerard's "analogical system" (1953, p. 172). Estévez tells us that *analog continuity* is a vital feature in our relationship with analog tools, one that reflects our physical and cognitive capacities and scalar boundaries. On the analog-human connection, she writes: "Steam powered trains or ships were analog machines, whose operation simulated processes that people had seen before in nature and in the functioning of their own bodies" (2009, p. 402). This is partly the mirroring concepts that we saw in Democritus, Aristotle, Gehlen and elsewhere. Note the phrase "processes that people had seen before in nature". Estévez follows up this point by remarking: "Moreover, their [analog technologies'] activity crosses time-space in a *visible way* that allows us to *grasp the link* between a movement and its effect, the process, the continuity" (pp. 402–403). So "continuity" and being able to grasp the visible link in, say, the workings of the journalistic process suggest a recognisable *presence of contiguity* in the creation of what Anderson describes as community. How might this work? "Community" in the context of Anderson's print capitalism was a mediated one. The characteristics of the technology determined its time-space (scalar) capacities. Modern communities were formed and mediated by print. Moreover, these were "inherently limited" (1983, p. 6) by the ideas contained in the information that they produced and shared. Anderson's "imagined communities" were also political and national communities, whose shared ideas were imagined principally from newspapers, books and pamphlets. For the literate population, the bulk of this came from newspapers because they were cheap and written for the readers' social demographic. This meant that Anderson's imagined communities read the same texts from newspapers, and these conveyed the same ideas about their "imagined world … [one that was] *visibly* rooted in everyday life" (pp. 35–36).

Anderson's "visibly" is italicised because it segues to Estévez's points about visibility and recognition in the analog process. In the time of print culture and print capitalism the increasingly complex means of distribution stretched the scalar links of "continuity" farther and farther afield, extending inexorably the imagined time-space of communities. Nonetheless, despite the ongoing challenges to our physical and cognitive scalar limits, for all of the 19th century and most of the 20th we were still able to "grasp the link" and the "continuity" of the process. For instance, the newspaper that travelled from London to the British settlement at Botany Bay in, say, 1815, announcing the defeat of Napoleon at Waterloo was not seen as a magical apparition by the colonialist reader but simply as recognition of the effect of the conveyance of the media by ship on a journey that had taken perhaps several months. The reader could imagine the world-scale traversal of time-space by a sailing ship halfway around the world because they could recognise the means of conveyance. And so, for all intents and purposes, the scale of the world was still human scaled and a process the reader could "grasp". As Richard Sennett put it in his book, *The Craftsman*, this consciousness in the modern period was still a materially based one because "we make sense of [its analog] functions by referring to our own human measure" (2009, p. 85). As the local public spheres of the 18th century expanded in to national and the international ones through the development of mass media then electronic media, including telegraph and television, our "human measure" stayed more or less the same. The time-space of the planet was compressing rapidly through those new technologies, but, right up until the age of McLuhan's 1960s "Global Village", the analog "measure" was *still* something recognisable. The Moon landing of 1969, to take one famous example, was an almost wholly analog affair. The continuous radio wave signals that beamed back to our televisions were still familiarly analog, and the awesome distance to the Moon was acknowledged by the perceptible time delays and fuzziness and overall baroqueness of its fusion of classical and what was now being called "high technology". And when Neil Armstrong floated down onto the Moon's surface, in a barely legible analog video representation, we could, even then, grasp what was going on in all its rococo weirdness. We were not yet dealing with digital near instantaneity and crystal clear and stable UHD LED screens.

3 Communication in the digital age
Truth and doubt

In his *Critique of Pure Reason* Immanuel Kant (1724–1804) derides as "ignorant" those who "took for granted, and presupposed, the nominal definition of truth, that it is the agreement of knowledge with its object" (2007, p. 90). Put like that—and ringing with the elitism and scepticism of the educated mid-18th-century philosopher—Kant pretty much condemns everyone, then and now, to the wretched category of the great uninformed reading public. Kant himself perceived truth in a more complex and ambiguous way, with truth shifting between empirical and transcendental forms, with reason and the individual cognitive capacities for knowledge acting as motive forces for what is, at root, a subjective process. For him, it would be naive to imagine that truth exists "out there" as something real and waiting to be revealed and relayed to the world by the journalist.

It is reasonable to suggest that up until the arrival of our digital postmodernity, most of the reading public, if they ever gave the matter any consideration, most likely thought differently about truth than did Kant. People read newspapers to be informed about something and "took for granted" that there was something real out there to be informed about. People understood that there were truths and there were lies existing in printed words. The perceptive abilities, or the prior knowledge of the engaged reader, was therefore more or less attuned to discerning one from the other. Johnson, in his *Dictionary*, listed several different definitions of "truth", and one he plucked from Shakespeare defines it as "purity from falsehood". Truth could therefore manifest as a simple binary, as in Johnson's characterisation. But in a semantic world of words and print produced through the sifting of the journalistic processes, the perception of truth was undergirded by a whole realm of human subjective and objective complexity—a process that nonetheless still sought to pair "knowledge with its object" in precisely the way the Kant rejected. Unlike the acquisition of language, humans are not hardwired to read; we need to learn it. And the "reading brain", as Maryanne Wolf terms it, is an instructible brain, a brain shaped and moulded by printed words that emanate from the "unnatural, cultural origin of literacy" (2018, p. 7). The scrutiny that the reading brain focuses upon the pages of the journalist's output is therefore freighted with

DOI: 10.4324/9781003054207-4

the learned assumptions of what years of reading and writing have instilled. Assumptions run in parallel with what reading also could impart to the literate mind, like cultural biases, political ideologies, the acceptance of a particular history or almost any narrative that seemed to support a certain truth. There is, for example, the mindset formed, in part, by a *faith* absorbed from the ultra-vatical pages of the Quran, the Torah, the Bible and countless interpretations of these. Away from faith-based texts, there are further and perhaps even less reasoned assumptions at play in the forms of reading that the brain imbibes to develop a sensitivity, an impression (an imprinting?) that suggests that what the sentences on the page say "feels right" and the *trust* that the feeling evokes can be echoed by the "ring of truth" that registers in the head in the transmission from page to brain.

Timothy Snyder, in his book *The Road to Unfreedom*, which looks at the new and infinitely more corrosive forms of propaganda and disinformation that digitality enables, writes that, "If there is no truth, there can be no trust" (2018, p. 281). The logic is reversible: if there is no trust then truth recedes behind a cloud of doubt, scepticism and sometimes fear. Snyder adds the caveat: "Final truth in this world is unattainable, but its pursuit leads the individual away from unfreedom" (p. 280). The form of public trust that is the positive effect of just such a "pursuit" of truth has taken a battering in recent times. Anthony Giddens, in his *Consequences of Modernity*, argues that "trust is a form of faith" (1990, p. 27), and these in their turn interact with public levels of confidence in social institutions, in the economy, in your own career prospects, in the material improvement of one's life and life chances, in political systems, in political parties, in individual politicians—and what you read in newspapers. Such processes of trust and faith, and the belief that there exists a truth to be found, were generated and circulated by the rhythms of modernity. Modernity brought many positive things in terms of social trust and cohesiveness, and, through these, the general "nominal definition of truth" that Kant distrusted was nonetheless able to become an intrinsic feature in the lifeworld of people as citizens. However, a complicating feature inherent to the structures of modernity is what Giddens terms "reflexivity". This stems from the "fact that social practices are constantly [being] examined and reformed in the light of incoming information about those very practices, thus constitutively altering their character" (p. 38). This procedure unfolds over time as an ongoing "revision of convention radicalised to apply (in principle) to all aspects of human life, including technological intervention into the material world" (p. 39). This is reason in action; a reason theoretically enabled to examine every aspect of modern life, "the freedom", as Kant put it, "to make public use of one's reason in all matters", and it constituted the core of his conception of what Enlightenment meant.

Reflexivity sounds positive: a form of reason that acts as a kind of collective self-checking, where mistakes or dangerous paths may be identified post facto or anticipated beforehand so to change course to make society more durable, predictable and trustworthy. As Giddens goes on to explain, however, reflexivity as a form of material action in the world may be deeply undermining of reason itself—and especially so in the spheres of science and technology. Drawing in part from the writings of Max Weber, Herbert Marcuse and Jacques Ellul, Giddens warns that in an industrial society, articulated by science and technology and driven by the profit motivations of capitalism, reflexivity becomes *instrumentalised.* Instrumentalisation refers to the rationalisation of tools and methods towards specific ends, and, as noted, since the Industrial Revolution this has been shaped by our old acquaintance the capitalist requirement for "efficiency" in production processes. In 1990, when Giddens developed his thesis of modernity, the "now largely instrumental relation between humans and the created environment" within a "harmful and unfettered scientific and technological development" was already, he acknowledged, a major problem, and one that "will have to be confronted" (p. 170). This has not happened, especially so in the "unfettered" development of technology from Silicon Valley or China's Zhongguancun technology hub, where products and processes are released indiscriminately into society with little or no understanding or concern as to how they will affect the economy, the culture and the mediated lives of individuals.

As we saw before, the path towards automation as a feature of "modernity" was taken by means of a growing instrumentalisation. Taking the human factor out of the technological forces of production, wherever possible, has been at the heart, not only of capitalist technology, but it is also the very essence of the computer logic that now drives both capitalism and technology innovation. The logic of digitally enabled automation has permeated and taken root in just about every sector of advanced societies. Automation, by way of its inherent purpose, *creates distance* between humans and production. And so, the "recognition" factor that is an essential element of the analogicity of humans begins to fade when "autonomous agents" inhabiting "closed world systems" (Johnston, 2010, p. 14), be they robots or automated processes, do the work *instead* of us (not for us). The subsequent inability for us to properly "grasp the link between a movement and its effect, the process, the continuity" (Estévez, 2009, pp. 402–403) means that automation increasingly serves to alienate and estrange instead of enlighten and include—with the latter pairing being the historical purpose of news media and journalism.

The *production* of information is journalism's raison d'être and its semantic source of truth and trust. This production process took a relatively unchanging analog form in the period of print capitalism. Today the digital *processing* of information, under which journalism mostly functions, is not an evolved system of speaking truth to power, or of ideological struggle, but merely the manifestation of the latest innovations in computation. These are systems of software and hardware produced by the need to automate and accelerate information in the service of economic and administrative and logistical "efficiency". Where does that leave trust and truth? Well, if a decline in trust in society indicates a crisis for truth, then to have some empirical measure of trust would give insight into the status of truth in our media world today. Francis Fukuyama, in his book *Trust,* writes about the links between technology and trust in developed societies. The mixture of anthropology and political economy he uses as his methodological approach is useful in giving a quantifiable grounding to the question. His book was written in 1995, the same year that Microsoft brought out its "game-changing" (Lilly, 2020) Windows 95 software, and so Fukuyama was rather perceptive in identifying the linkages between an emergent Internet and trust. He wrote: "Trust does not reside in integrated circuits or fibre optic cables. Although it involves an exchange of information, trust is not reducible to information" (1995, p. 25). Fukuyama locates trust in the idea of *social capital*—an idea floated by James Coleman (in 1988) and popularised in Robert Putnam's *Bowling Alone* (2000)—which Putnam defines as the "ability of people to work together for common purposes in groups and organisations" (p. 10). What is clear in these works is that trust, if it is reducible to anything at all, is reducible to humans, to people as creators of what Fukuyama, citing Putnam, calls "civic communities" (p. 99) that are held together by "bonds of trust" (p. 49).

Fukuyama's concept becomes more interesting for our purposes when his social capital, civic community and bonds of trust are interpolated with an idea discussed previously—analog scale. This suggests that the production and durability of trust and therefore truth are different in analog and digital societies. We saw that modernity was more or less human-scaled and based upon the analog technologies that reflected our human cognitive and physical potentials and limitations when they functioned in society. An analogical reading of Fukuyama suggests that "civic communities" and their "bonds of trust" have a human-scalar and therefore analog quality that has been overlooked. Fukuyama's technique is designed to measure levels of trust that exist within communities. He creates two categories: low-trust and high-trust communities. Trust is low or in decline in communities where social capital in the form of "neighbourhoods, churches, unions, clubs, and charities" exhibit the "general sense … of a lack of shared values and community with those around them" (p. 11). Trust is higher in communities "with the strongest internal ties" and these would typically "have the weakest bonds with those [communities] outside" (p. 154). In other words, the more integrated and internally connected a community, the higher the levels of trust within them and, presumably, these more cohesive communities would have lower reserves of trust for those outside their own acknowledged and recognised community. So to extend the hypothesis of our human analogicity to the idea of trust and truth, in terms of human scale as a way to contextualise low-trust and high-trust communities, analog dominant societies are more conducive to producing higher levels of trust and perceptions of truth in ways that distributed and networked societies—digital societies—are not.

The forms of community generated by digitality like the numberless communities that exist in and through social media, could be said to be highly integrated themselves, with strong internal ties, and so high levels of trust (and therefore shared perceptions of truth) could feasibly live within them. However, such communities are *digital scale* and inevitably shaped by the technology that creates them and so the discontinuous logic of digital will tend to reproduce certain characteristics: single-issue communities that focus on lifestyle choices and interests, identity awareness and promotion, and these may be indifferent or unreceptive to the ideas and values of the more universalist and public institutions that have roots in modern forms of analog civil society. The super-rationalising effects of social media algorithms attract individuals who may be shaped by their communicative logic into certain forms of community that can be, to borrow Judith Butler's phrasing: "factionalising, identitarian, and particularistic" (Butler, 1998, p. 33). The danger is that their trust is restricted to their associates, and their truths likewise subject mostly to their own internal scrutiny and validation. The products of journalism will likely have only limited effect upon these in the construction and maintenance of a public sphere.

This exploratory take on the nature of digital truth and trust seeks to understand the generative forces that shape and maintain them through mediation—through the forms of technology that create them, the "communication networks that enable thought to have social existence" (Debray, 2007, p. 5). The analog-digital dualism lets us see truth and trust in a new light for our new times. In respect of the "imagined communities" that technology enables, the concept suggests that digital media detaches people from sources of news media information in ways that analog media didn't and couldn't. Digital produces discontinuous and highly diverse data through platform-based accumulation and distribution to individuals and communities created by patented algorithmic code (Srnicek, 2017 Striphas, 2015). Newspapers survive by contributing to this, and their print content increasingly goes online. They link to, or are co-opted by, immense distributed flows of global news, entertainment, opinion, hyperlinks, newsfeeds, blogs and smaller platforms like X and individual ones like Substack. Inevitably, then, online newspapers and the journalists who write content for them have a very large presence in the digital sphere, but the characteristics of digital serves mostly to distance the newspaper and journalist from the reader and from the online communities that the reader may be part of (see Earp & McChesney, 2013). Taken as part of a general process, the fracturing, the dissociation and the tendency to reduce journalistic narratives to bite-sized chunks of data "discontinuous and quantized" (Gerard, 1953, p. 181) places news media and journalism in an invidious position with an online public in the context of trust and truth. Analog scaling-up to a size where even globally shared public opinion or discussion is possible, such as was evident in the Moon landing—is rendered impossible at *any* level of scale through the digital architecture of postmodern news production and consumption, where scale is measured in individual clicks instead of shared consciousness.

We see measurably declining levels of public trust recorded in polls and surveys reaching back over several decades. And in recent times the problems of dissociated and insulated online communities are paralleled by an explosion of digitally enabled misinformation, disinformation, deep-fakes and cheap-fakes and has deepened public mistrust of both mass-media and the journalists who produce its content. In the United States, Gallup conducted a longitudinal study from 1972 until 2022 (Brenan, 2022). It found that 1974 was a year of heightened media attention on the Watergate scandal and the *Washington Post* investigations into lies and coverups emanating from the Nixon White House. Then, around 70 per cent of respondents had a "great deal/fair amount" of trust in newspapers, TV and radio. Levels of trust reached its highest point around this time, ticking up from the base year of 1972. Those whose trust levels measured "none at all" was then under 5 per cent, down even further from the base year. That was as good as it got for both categories. Trust levels began a trend downward to reach 34 per cent in 2020; and mistrust levels went steadily upwards, reaching an all-time high of 38 per cent in 2022. Pew Research gives nuance to the stark graph lines drawn by Gallup. A 2022 Pew survey found that alongside the known fact that "trust [in news media] is declining" (Pew, 2022), digital misinformation is also seen as a big driver of attitudes, "with a large share of Americans saying that made-up news creates confusion and is a really big problem for society" (Pew, 2022). Most significant for our purposes in the Pew analysis is the comment that: "Americans don't trust each other the way they used to. They don't think they share the same facts that they used to". Accordingly: "their trust has become *disaggregated and divided*" (Pew, 2022).

A different but related perspective is revealed in the same Pew report that finds that most journalists themselves believe that social media is "having a negative impact upon journalism as a whole", with almost 70 per cent of those surveyed saying that digital forms and processes are having a "very" or "somewhat" negative affect on their profession (Pew, 2022). Journalists are mostly compelled to use social media to remain in employment. It is foisted upon them as an "efficiency" and "productivity" tool, following the business model ideology that began in Wapping in 1986, with Rupert Murdoch threatening to fire anyone who refused to use the new computerised tools of the trade (Macintyre, 2016). Moreover, social media tools put journalists in direct competition with each other—not for the exclusive interview, or the scoop on official corruption or malfeasance, but for clicks and likes and the hope for traction that will capture readers' "attention" data that can be collected and sold online by their employers to advertisers. Power has shifted in newsrooms, in the Anglosphere at any rate, where employers have been able to push through digitalisation in most aspects of production and distribution. And journalists, like everyone else, have had to learn new skills and to *become dependent* upon them to do new forms of work. Old deadlines based upon print schedules are now 24/7 deadlines to have content always or almost ready to upload. Journalists need to be able to respond to "events" occurring online as well as off, whilst keeping abreast of a never-ending stream of notifications about "developments" on X, on Telegram, as well as what the competition are up to in respect of breaking news. The acceleration of the temporal life of the journalist's work means that there is less time to do the more time-consuming labour. It is a zero-sum game. Time scrolling on X is time deducted from reflecting, analysing, cogitating on an issue. Short-cuts become an inevitability, and they lead to poor working practices like "churnalism" (Davies, 2008), where resort by the journalist to simply recycle wire service copy and press releases from companies or government agencies becomes a temptation—unavoidable for some, an acquired habit for others.

Faith in truth: a foundation of modern journalism

The idea of truth that seized early modern journalism, and the one still prevalent today, is a particular one. And as in much else, the idea was shaped by the forces of its time, by the mental conceptions that gained traction in the social, political and intellectual fervour that characterised the 18th century. The Enlightenment movement, as noted, was the primary intellectual and political force that inculcated the ideas that sought to change the world by applying them to the world. Although journalist-agitators like Thomas Paine wanted to "begin the world over again" (Paine, 2012, p. 85), to sweep away everything associated with the *ancien regime*, aspects of culture and history are not so readily eradicated. The Enlightenment, for all its emphasis on the new thinking pushing aside the old, important elements of the "modern" thinking were already present in Christian doctrine—present in theory at least. Moreover, some important traditional Christian ideas suffused the thinking of many of the proposers and carriers of Enlightenment values themselves. This included the idea that "truth" is something real that may be found. "The truth is in the Bible" is a common sentiment in Christian doctrine and carried over into Enlightenment thought in the form of there being objective truths to be found by way of reason and free-thinking. Kant, the sceptic of a "nominal" truth, still hoped that a more fully developed Enlightenment would discover what he called the "hidden truth" that would be revealed in both its empirical and its transcendental forms under a broader criterion of modern knowledge. But in his time "a great deal was still lacking" concerning the perceived nature of truth and had to be corrected before the "age of enlightenment" could become "an enlightened age"—an important semantic distinction for Kant upon which much rested.

Kant's "enlightened age" never came, and the Enlightenment, more broadly, underwent devastating critiques (Nietzsche, 1996: Adorno & Horkheimer, 2002) as well as many spirited defences (e.g., Todorov, 2010).

Nonetheless, in the practical, material world, the "nominal" conception of truth survived. And journalists, from the time of the Enlightenment until recently, wrote under the assumption that they, by way of their reporting, were describing the truths they found; and readers similarly assumed that what they read was a form of words on paper that corresponded to a truth, a reality—or at least it purported to be because it was printed. Statements on paper corresponded to a reality in the world, and this was how truth and knowledge existed and circulated in a mediated, print culture world. Kant imagined that this degraded form of truth, the "agreement of knowledge with its object" (2007, p. 90) was only half the story. But it's a story that has not only retained the loyalty of the journalist class and the mass public they wrote for, but also for most philosophers, too. Marian David (2015) cites a 200-person survey of faculty in 99 leading philosophy departments that found that 50.8 per cent of them accept what is known as the "correspondence theory" of truth. As David writes: "This fits with the observation that typically, discussions of the nature of truth take some version of the correspondence theory as the default view, the view to be criticized or to be defended against criticism" (David, 2015). And so the religious- and Enlightenment-derived nature of truth as having specific characteristics still has a strong adherence in the popular mind and underpins the value system and ethical code of journalists as much today as it did in the 18th century. Yet is it still able to function effectively on that old, modern basis in the postmodern, post-print digital age?

Truth and power: from analog to digital mediation

In *The Rights of Man*, Thomas Paine imagined that changing the world was a matter of ideas being given material reality by writing and by the sheer force of will: "The mind of the nation had changed … and the new order of things has naturally followed the new order of thoughts" (2018, p. 63). Truth could be found, therefore, by the adoption of a "new order of thoughts"—presumably his. The 1776 U.S. Declaration of Independence, which Paine helped bring about, enumerated five "truths" ("that all men are created equal", etc.) that were held to be "self-evident". These were "self-evident" because they were "discovered" through Enlightenment reason and given vatical authority by the fact of their being written down, "Adopted and Printed" as the *Declaration* says, on the Fourth of July, with "copies printed by John Dunlap and … dispatched by members of Congress to various committees, assemblies, and to the commanders of the Continental troops". This was how truth was established in times of revolution.

And this was Elizabeth Eisenstein's print culture in analog action. It was politics, ideas, media and war mixed up in struggles over the nature and outcomes of revolutionary social change. But Benedict Anderson's insistence on print capitalism as a more accurate descriptor was the acknowledgement of the economic aspect of the Enlightenment, too, and how, especially after the

Industrial Revolution got going, the logic of capitalism as a shaper of reality and therefore the nature of truth was not a perspective upon truth that Kant or Paine or any of the *philosophes* of the time could have contemplated or anticipated. Not until Marx, nearly a century later, would we see a systematic description and critique of the role of capital and the effect that capitalist power would have upon ideas and politics and therefore on reality and truth. Indeed, acting as a journalist-correspondent for the *New York Tribune*, Marx would adapt his political economy analysis to tell his reader the new "truths" about such events as British rule in India, the Opium War and the "fact" that the American Civil War was based upon vital economic struggles over such things as trade, competition, access to raw materials, markets and the exploitation of slave labour. With the growth of industry and capitalism, truth and politics quickly became linked in the shaping of reality. Print capitalism was its herald by means of a mass media that became fully fledged around the turn of the 20th century and provided the major narratives that reflected the political interests of the capital-institutional nexus.

The dialectic between truth and politics is one where it may more accurately be described as between truth and *power*, with power fought over in the struggles between institutional politics and a dynamic capitalism. The journalist and the media were thus placed *between* truth and power as the investigators and narrators of truth as it is reflected in the face of the powers that created reality. This logic had solidified into what Hannah Arendt called the "common species of rational truth" (1967, p. 2), i.e., the correspondence between knowledge and its object. And it became the accepted rationality at the heart of the journalistic ethos for most of the 20th century. After the Second World War, what had become a Western system of organised mass media based on the Fordist model, gave recognisable and powerful structure to its established narratives. However, this perceived phase of stability in the development of Western power, a period David Harvey dubbed "high Fordism" (1989, p. 140), would last only a few decades, from the 1940s until the 1970s, reaching an apex in the 1960s. And by the end of that decade and beginning in the 1970s, a tectonic transformation in the operations of capitalism would have a profound effect upon the nature of truth and its legitimacy.

Arendt's doubts about the nature of truth within Enlightenment modernity never went away. In her essay "Truth and Politics" she argued that if the concept of truth is a lie, then it is a lie that we need to have. She describes the philosophical problem: "The modern age, which believes that truth is neither given to nor disclosed to but produced by the human mind" fluctuates between the "common species of rational truth" and "factual truth" (1967, p. 2). Both rational and factual forms are affected by the struggles between truth and power. And it was a struggle that was played out in many ways through analog mass media. Arendt's "modern age" and Harvey's "high Fordism", one the expression of an ideology, the other of a productive force, involved the masses and their media. Raymond Williams took a keen interest in the tension between the mass media and the masses. As a Marxist writing on media, culture and literary theory, Williams saw a distinctly asymmetrical power relation oriented towards the manipulation and exploitation of the masses. In his 1958 *Culture and Society*, Williams saw society, in this era of Fordism and regulation, and with mature forms of mass media, as being a more deeply administered one, where conceptions of truth and the exercise of power were concentrated sufficiently to organise society mainly to the benefit of the capital-political institutional nexus, where the "masses", the people the journalist writes for, are formed in a specific way, for specific reasons:

> The conception of persons as masses springs, not from an inability to know them, but from the interpretation of them according to a formula. [...] The formula, in fact, will proceed from our intention. If our purpose is art, education, the giving of information or opinion, our interpretation will be in terms of the rational and interested being. If, on the other hand, our purpose is manipulation—the persuasion of a large number of people to act, feel, think, know, in certain ways—the convenient formula will be that of the masses.
>
> (1958, p. 322)

Williams always saw potential in the working class *as a class*, but he also acknowledged that a politics of consciousness, of workers seeing the "truth" of themselves as a class, had to be a prerequisite for positive social or revolutionary change. The failure of this consciousness, such as it was, in the social upheavals of the 1960s set in train an intellectual disenchantment with much of the Enlightenment legacy. Herbert Marcuse (1898–1979) was one such thinker. He saw a "one-dimensional society", one created by ever more powerful technological administration and enabled by ineffectual media and journalism, where the real interests of people are never shown to them as possibilities (2002, pp. 3–87). Consequently, the "truths" people seek, Marcuse believed, are shallow ones, expressed as material needs and wants—with capitalism willing to supply and reinforce through advertising. He saw a "commodity culture" where "exchange value, not truth value counts" (p.61). Marcuse also saw a "closing of the universe of discourse" (pp. 87–126) where the "quest for the meaning of words" (p. 74) is a battle that the masses in the mass society were losing.

Losing not appearing as losing was something Marcuse and others were critically attuned to. Enlightenment truth as mediated through highly advanced (and still analog) mass media was problematic (at least) for a philosopher like Jean Baudrillard (1929–2007) in his 1983 *In the Shadow of the Silent Majorities*. For him, the masses of the post-1960s era no longer needed or wanted a political or intellectual class, journalists and newspapers included, to show them what their needs and wants were. They knew. The masses had themselves *become a medium* in the McLuhanesque sense, and their message was spectacle, distraction, sport, tabloid media and more *images as opposed to writing*. As Tiziana Terranova puts it in her *Network Culture*, Baudrillard's disturbing thesis expressed the "spectacularization of communication and hence the spectacularization of politics" (2004, pp. 135–136). This was something not imposed on the masses, as Williams would have it in the 1950s, but was:

> demanded by the formation of a mass. The masses are not specific social classes, but more of a generalized dynamics that takes over when you take away all attributes, predicates, qualities or references from a large number of people.

Building on Baudrillard's thesis, Terranova points to a difficulty this raises for "journalists who subscribe to a professional ethics rooted in a liberal modernity" (p. 16). Truth and truth values are unable to resonate with or break through to masses who know what they want and what they need—masses that demand it through media forms and processes (and sources of power) that do not need to manipulate them but make their profits from them by giving them what they think they want.

This is an instance of the so-called post-structuralist turn, something well underway when Baudrillard wrote *In the Shadow*. His thesis on the "implosion of meaning in the media" (pp. 95–112) arose from a general feeling, especially in the French and American humanities departments, that the meanings that structuralism argued as being set deep within semantic structures and systems (e.g., Barthes, 1968) no longer held their explanatory power. New electronic media functioning as new vectors of meaning exploded structuralism's assumptions of a self-contained and stable system of meaning. The literary theory roots of post-structuralism, beginning with Jacques Derrida (1967), a converted Roland Barthes (1968) and others, spread out to incorporate the concepts of Michel Foucault (1977), who, along with disenchanted post-Marxists like Jean-François Lyotard (1979) and Gilles Deleuze (1983), began to see the world very differently from the inheritors of a badly bruised Enlightenment legacy. That project was seen to have gone the way of instrumental rationality and had run amok with the Nazi creation of the death factories and the U.S. development of the atomic bomb. By the end of the 1960s the general fracturing of Enlightenment certainties was both cause and consequence of more technologically mediated and fragmented forms of reality and truth. What McLuhan and Baudrillard termed the "image", and Guy Debord named the "spectacle", began to prevail over words and writing as the new "discourses" that generated their own "regimes of truth"—truths that were more explicitly man-made expressions and disseminations of particular power interests (Foucault, 1977, p. 13).

Journalism could not avoid the realities of a new postmodern, post-structuralist world. Language, words and media, the journalist's stock in trade, were no longer so securely rooted in a close and widely acknowledged correspondence between knowledge and its object. However, it nevertheless kept on *acting as if it was,* writing with the same print culture tools of the newspaper industry but now competing with electronic media—and primarily the socially transformative technology of local and globalised television.

Examples of the eclipse of journalistic power are numerous. The one is chosen here is a kind of origin story of the long decline of the status of print culture and print capitalism as sources of truth-finding and truth-telling within Western societies. The idea of truth as being somehow represented in the authority of the word—especially the printed word—was already in crisis in the early 1960s. Mass media as the main transmitter of journalistic practice was already under competitive pressure. Television as a textual practice prompted new forms of subjectivity in the reader and novel ways of understanding the world. Its message was more fluid and absorbing, and, like mobile phones in our own time, was immediately attractive to consumers. Television constituted a new "practice of truth" that was more compelling and less cognitively demanding than print. The correspondence between knowledge and its object is based upon a dynamic "image ecology" (Terranova, 2004, p. 144), and it gives consumers a different space of reading and decoding that printed news could not provide. Journalism and print faced a serious challenge, and what follows shows how journalism tried to adapt to the new (and still analog) realities. However, in the end, journalism succeeded mainly in diminishing further its status as modern "truth-teller" in a world that was leaving modernity and its traditional conceptions of truth behind. The example is not a precursor of what today has been labelled our "post-truth era", but more the beginnings of a proliferation of different modes of truth and ways of expressing them across many professions and through increasingly effective forms of communication—from the newspaper to the Internet.

In 1966 Truman Capote published *In Cold Blood*, a book that was something of a sensation. It combined fact with fiction and left the reader to fill in the gaps of truth and morality. These issues were explored in the book through literary techniques, such as the "intercutting of different story strands, intense close-ups, flashbacks, traveling shots, background detail, all as if [Capote] were fleshing out a scenario" (Kaufman, 1966). The author merged the literary with the journalistic to create what was, in essence, a new form of communication, where fact and truth took on a more ambiguous appearance. *In Cold Blood* was an example of what fellow novelist Tom Wolfe dubbed "new journalism" (1973). Centred around the 1959 killings of four members of the Clutter family in a farmhouse in rural Kansas, Capote attended the trial, interviewed the two men accused, and then wrote an account of it after their conviction and execution in 1965. Capote brought journalism into the work to give his story a real-event basis, but he also used a technique he described as "historical non-fiction" with deliberate purpose: to better compete against the market threat of television for telling stories to a mass audience. The journalist Clay Felker, a founding editor of *New York* magazine, rationalised the motivation behind this and similar new journalism, writing: "we had to do something TV couldn't do" (Nicholson, 1976, p. 57). The literary critic Dwight McDonald was less accommodating. He called such experimentation with the representation of truth, "Parajournalism—a bastard form exploiting the factual authority of journalism and the atmospheric license of fiction" (Nicholson, 1976, p. 55). Whichever way you view it, a new "practice of truth" was born with this kind of writing. It was a mutation of the form of journalism. It was still linked to the Enlightenment ethic of journalism, but it allowed truth and responsibility to float free from knowledge and its object.

The "new journalism" example shows that television was perceived as a serious threat to printed mass media and its classical expressions of modernity in both news and literature. However, from its inception television was a consumer durable and not necessarily a new force for a new public sphere. And as a consumer durable it quickly became a consumer choice, becoming part of a more suburban lifestyle, a "privatisation" of the public sphere into which individuals could retreat and be entertained. On the face of it, television, as another media choice, could coexist with print media news. Consumers could take both and consume both even as one influenced the other such that they became alike. As television become increasingly widespread and dominant, newspapers, in the effort to compete and survive, took on aspects of television forms where it could. And so text space began to make room on the page for more pictures. These were stills but were nonetheless attractive to the eye of a 20th-century consumer visually trained to photographs. But this was print undermining itself: a written accompaniment to the photograph could easily find itself describing the picture as much, if not more, as it described the news event. "A picture can speak a thousand words" runs the platitude, but it is no less apposite because of that. The picture writes the story for the harried and time-pressed journalist. Reflection and analysis are thus easily sacrificed at the altar of shallow description. Over the decades, this was a largely unnoticed process, yet the pictorialising of news represented another degree of abstraction of the writing from the reporting of the news event itself.

Digital technology represents a further degree of abstraction for journalism and its practice of writing. Journalism's writing is the basis of its art where, in the actual hands of actual journalists, stories could be skilfully and painstakingly crafted such that they could "resonate" with readers, individual and collective, and sometimes change things, for better or for worse. Such journalism, an art as much as it is a learned technique, still happens, of course. And the narratives produced, be they about political policies, judicious editorialising, institutional corruption, insightful analysis, hypocrisies in boardrooms, murder most foul or outstanding bread-and-butter commentary, still has an audience. But does it make much difference anymore? If "quality" journalism is increasingly paywalled, banishing those millions unable or willing to pay, then who are their stories addressed to, apart from an IP address? The digital time-space is antithetical to the modern kind of journalism. And it has become diminished by an all-powerful digital capitalism and the segmented and fractured "public" it has generated. Platform's such as Meta or Amazon or Google are powerful news publishers, even if their owners are unwilling to admit the fact. Hundreds of millions read their free online news of various types for various reasons. However, for these, expectations and assumptions regarding journalistic ethics and public sphere participation probably don't figure as highly in what are now highly unstable markets of attention, clicks, advertising and mis/dis-information. Nevertheless, many others choose to enter the paywall or buy the printed copy with their more traditional expectations and assumptions more or less intact. Some of their prefigurations, one conjectures, may have to do with a rejection of "message news" (Meek, 2023) and a trust that, whatever they trouble to read as news, is knowledge corresponding to fact in some plausible way. Moreover, and connectedly, the actual *writing of the story* is a key part of the motivation and a clue as to why journalism, as an essentially analog profession, has not yet succumbed to analog obscurity.

Writing *as narrative*, then, is worth considering in our analysis of the analog essence of humans and the role of journalism in a digital-dominated world. How do narratives work? What are we losing in their relative demise? And what would a public sphere be like without the art of narrative making and without narrative readers who make sense of their world through them?

4 Journalism as narrative and practice

What's the story?

Creating stories in the form of narratives is what journalists do when they put sentences together. Today, journalists still write stories, some short and some long, some better than others, and the conscientious journalist will always seek to improve this most important element of the profession. But to say that stories are the essence of what journalists do is rather obvious. Like the obviousness of writing to literate readers, it is something we take for granted and to which we give little consideration. However, the relative invisibility of the importance of narratives means that their decline as the primary form of journalistic communication has been incorporated almost unnoticed into our mediated lives. This has important consequences both for journalism as a profession and for an engaged community as public sphere.

The aim here is to make salient the theory and practice of narrative writing in the communicative life of humans. We begin with some framing questions posed by journalist-academic Martin McQuillan in an edited collection on narrative theory where he writes:

> What if there were no more stories? What if stories, contrary to narrative theory's fundamental article of faith (that narrative, like love, is all around us), were coming, or had already come, to an end? How would we know? What would we do?
>
> (2000, p. 2)

In the public sphere today something else is "all around us". It is a different type of narrative. It comes from journalists, but it comes also from potentially anyone with a computer and Internet connection. Those were not the stories that were still being published as the dominant form at the early age of the Internet when McQuillan wrote. Those were the stories of classical print culture—and they are now the minority. What is "all around us" is very different form narrative and it dominates a very different public sphere. The digital networks that journalism operates within today produce what James Meek (2023) describes as "message news". This is an "efficient" short form

DOI: 10.4324/9781003054207-5

of communication that's eminently suited to the affordances of digital logic, but it is one that helps to overturn two hundred and fifty years of analog journalism and the modernity it helped create. The cause and effect of "message news" will be the subject of the next chapter but, to continue, let us contemplate the concept of classical narrative and its centrality to the practice of classical journalism.

In Evelyn Waugh's celebrated 1937 satire, *Scoop*: *A Novel about Journalists*, there is a scene where Corker, a Fleet Street journalist, and William Boot, also a journalist but for a rival newspaper, the *Daily Beast*, are in a hotel in the fictional East African country of Ismailia, discoursing on the peculiarities of their profession. Corker to Boot:

> You know, you've got a lot to learn about journalism. Look at it this way. News is what a chap who doesn't care much about anything wants to read. And it's only news until he's read it. After that it's dead. We're paid to supply news. If someone else has sent a story before us, our story isn't news.

This parody on the cynicism and world-weariness of a certain kind of mass-media journalist, one looking mainly for the sensational story to further their career as opposed to performing a public service, was an instant and lasting success for Waugh. It was primarily because its depictions of hard-bitten journalistic contempt for professional ethics seemed close to reality. It was a perspective that Christopher Hitchens repeated in his "Introduction" to a reissue of *Scoop*, published in 2000. Hitchens wrote that: "*Scoop* endures because it is a novel of pitiless realism" (2000, p. vi). Hitchens knew something about journalism, and doubtless his summation still had some traction at the time of his writing. However, the assumed timeless quality of modern journalism was then undergoing its own "pitiless" transformation through technological change. This would quickly consign any residual "realism" of *Scoop* to the historical dustbin. Today *Scoop* no longer "endures" as a parable for the profession in the present time but has become instead a relic from a bygone age of mass-media newspapers.

To understand the fate of modern journalism and the stories that were once the structure and contextualisation of news, we need to understand the fate of the narrative as a basic structure of human communication.

Narrative as vector for truth and reality

The study of narrative concentrates broadly within the humanities, in literary theory, in cultural theory and analysis and in anthropology. The practical concerns of narrative, however, involve the individual in almost every aspect of life. Barbara Hardy imagined the psychology of narrative structure as being immanent in everything we do. She writes that "we dream in narrative, daydream in narrative, remember, anticipate, hope, despair, believe, doubt, plan, revise, criticise, construct, gossip, learn, hate and love by narrative"' Hardy goes on to note: "In order to really live, we make up stories about ourselves and others, about the personal as well as about the social past and future" (Hardy, 1968, p. 5). This is instructive and is something most of us would feel at the subjective level. The "really live" phraseology is also important. Narratives connect us to what we sense as the reality of our lives and of the wider world. Moreover, it is by means of narrativisation or telling a story that "truth", or knowledge corresponding to its object, is transmitted through either oral or written communication. Jerome Bruner argues that narratives and narrative comprehension within the human psyche act as a "form of not only representing but of constituting reality" (Bruner, 1991, p. 5). Bruner notes also that the force of narrative upon the psyche, and the human receptivity to narrative power acting as an orienting, cohering and validating force, begins in early childhood. "There is compelling evidence to indicate," he writes, "that narrative comprehension is among the earliest powers of mind to appear in the young child and the most widely used forms of organising human experience" (Bruner, 1991, p. 9). That our receptivity to narrative is deep-set and ancient suggests that these "earliest powers of the mind" are bound up with our initial relationship with writing and reading. And so, just as the act of writing and reading of the written word enabled the formation of consciousness, as suggested by Walter Ong (1982), then so too did narrative become technologised (as distinct from being purely oral) and encoded with the bio- and eco-*temporalities* of writing. The temporal aspect of narrative is important, and we will say more about this shortly in the context of journalistic storytelling.

To continue, storied news is what evolved from the human-analog practice of writing that journalists used right up until the digital age. It evolved through the process of writing itself and, further, through print and print culture. The writing production process infused the words on newsprint pages with the vatic characteristics of authority, of truth-telling, and acted more or less as representative of knowledge corresponding with its subject. Ong tells us that printed words had the effect of organising and "controlling" the earlier form of narrative that existed in oral cultures, where stories were prone to mutation in the telling and retelling of them (1982, p. 130). Adapted and extended from oral narratives by means of the technologised word, writing created its own fixed narrative structures that would be replicated accurately and without limit in print. And the power of writing on the page, as we have seen previously, would transfer this "control" to the reading subject. Alan Singer is more specific about this point, saying that narrative writing "determines a position for the [individual] to inhabit" and who "submits to the contingencies of that determination" (1983, p. 30). Singer maintains that not only does the structure of the story shape our understanding of the communication, but also that the narrative is itself shaped by its technological structuring.

So, what are the structural features of narrative? Narrative theory is a wide and deep area of study, spanning structuralist and post-structuralist writers and theories from Roland Barthes and Jacques Derrida to Claude Lévi-Strauss and Jean-François Lyotard, to name only a few notables. To allow us to move forward, however, the diverse features of narrative theory are here distilled down to the very common basics and are those judged most useful to illuminate the processes of journalism. First, narrative stories have, in broad terms, a beginning, which introduces the problem or topic or issue; a middle, which reveals the main or important features of the story that moves to a climax; and then an end, in which some sort of resolution or conclusion is offered. Films and novels often work closely to this structure. Journalists would use this form mostly as a guiderail to keep the reader following the story in the way to which they have been culturally trained. Second, modern narratives usually follow a linear unfolding where the story progresses through time in the same way that the reader would in their subjective life. As J. Hillis Miller put it, "Word follows word from beginning to end" in a way that the "the reader follows or is supposed to follow" (2000, pp. 231–232). This strong direction is achieved by means of the controlling effect that written words have, and that literacy inculcates into the reader by way of unconscious expectation of how the process is supposed to flow. The flow may be broken up in journalism by photographs or charts or advertisements or whatever, but in ways and with effects that don't disturb the linearity (p. 232). A newspaper report, even a long-form piece, would rarely disturb the linearity by means of, say, repetition or through forms of words that, Miller citing Paul Ricoeur, "curve back on itself, recross itself, tie itself in knots" (p. 232). Such deviation would merely serve to exasperate or confound the reader. Third, plot is another form of control in that it is a linear cause-and-effect ordering of narrative via words that unfold the story from beginning to end in a *time sequence*. For example, a journalist might narrate the events of a street demonstration by describing the mood of a gathering crowd at a certain place, the presence of any notable people or organisations, the attitude of the police, the march to a rallying point and any dramatic events such as speeches, violence, arrests, dispersal, etc. Again, common literacy trains the reader to expect events to unfold temporally in a certain sequence. These core elements of narrative will have numberless variations. However, in terms of the reader's effective engagement with the technology and corresponding to what was argued previously through the work of Silvia Estévez (2009), the inherent analog dimension of the necessary human *recognition* of what the technology is doing is always present, despite the possible variations in narrative expression.

The controlling effect of narrative storytelling has another major effect that impinges directly and negatively upon the capacity for classical modern journalism to function in the digital age and that, as just touched on, is temporality. Mechanical clock time functioned as the rhythm of modernity. It is the organising and coordinating element that gives capitalism and modern life the predictability necessary to be a practicable system (see Kern, 1983). The clock is also a way to measure and regulate humans in their objective behaviours and actions. Being controlled by the objective time of the clock, however, means that something more subjective and diverse in humans is sublimated—and that is the individual experience of time. This is a consciousness-based form of temporality that is suppressed, but not effaced, by the moving hands on a clock face. Phenomenologists such as Henri Bergson and Edmund Husserl called it duration. It was Bergson who coined the term *la durée* to describe the experience of time as being a flow of moments a "succession without distinction" as opposed to the mechanical unfolding of successive and discrete instants as measured through the clock (Bergson, 1950, p. xi). Conscious time experience passes from the past to the present and into the future, and process or reflection, the experience of the present and projections into the future that Husserl called "retention" (moments perceived from the past), and "protention" (moments that have not yet become but are linked to the experience of the living present) (Husserl, 1964, p. 110).

By way of Walter Ong we have seen already that writing transforms consciousness. Narrative storytelling through writing is no different in this respect. Christain Metz, in his "Notes Toward a Phenomenology of the Narrative" tells us something important about the magic spell the classical journalist once cast with print. He writes: "By its very existence, the narrative suppresses the *now* … or the here" (2000, p. 89) (italics in original), meaning that an attentive or relatively close reading (a narrative storyline) of an event somewhere in the world has the dreamlike effect of transporting the subjective consciousness of the reader out from the time-space of their own particular present and in to the abstracted world invoked by the words they are reading. Leafing through the pages of a newspaper, the reader can become immersed in the various stories and experience emotions of amusement, anger, schadenfreude, empathy, etc. rising from the words and images on a sheet of paper. The subjective time of the "now", the present that the individual lives as a fleshly analog being, is suspended—frozen—through the controlling engagement with the newspaper and its stories. The medium itself, indeed, generated its own meta-temporality through the schedules of capitalist modernity. Dailies (sometimes morning, afternoon and evening editions), weeklies and monthlies imposed their artificial calendarisation upon the subjective consciousness of the modern print culture reader. Trust, authority and knowledge corresponding to its object, all expressed through narrative, made for a powerful print media effect that helped shape the minds, attitudes and belief-systems that oriented the reader in the world. This was a modern political world, a civil society and public sphere where the "imagined communities" of party, nation, ethnicity, history and present and future contrived a highly mediated worldview. By means of the power of the word over consciousness, this abstract world seemed logical, coherent and seemingly natural to the print-trained literate person. Moreover, it represented something real and tangible—a mass-media readership of objectivised and abstracted people who nonetheless could feel connected to one other.

Graphosphere to videosphere: politics and media in transition from modernity to postmodernity

The ideal-typical newspaper reader just described, one trained and immersed in the controlling long-form narratives penned by the journalist and distributed metronomically by mechanical-industrial publishing systems, reached an apex of effect as modern mass media over the late 1960s. This was the endpoint of Régis Debray's "vast arc of time" that stretched "from 1448 to around 1968: from the Gutenberg Revolution to the rise of TV" (2007, pp. 5–6). Emphasising the French context from which his theory emerged, Debray continues: "The cycle comes to an end in the aftermath of May 1968, Year One of the videosphere" (p. 6). The decade or so after 1968 was something of a transitional phase in the context of Western mass media, one in which the newspaper-television combined effect had a historic role in the public sphere/fourth estate shaping of a landmark postwar event: the war in Vietnam, which we will come to presently.

As far as journalistic Enlightenment values are concerned, the contribution to this phase of postwar geopolitical turmoil was significant. The May 1968 *événements* that Debray refers to were symptomatic of a general crisis of modernity; the beginning of the end of an upward trend of the postwar articulations of Enlightenment humanism and reason, and the progress made in the anti-colonial and national liberation struggles since 1945. "Year One of the videosphere" didn't necessarily mean the death of the graphosphere in France or anywhere else. A *fusion* between newspapers and television was still able to produce an Enlightenment impulse on a vast and collective scale. It was most prominently in 1968 France, however, that the promise of modernity was beginning to be seen, as Guy Debord termed it, as a "bad dream", from which many were beginning to awaken from (2014, p. 7).

The growing rationalisation of capitalism was provoking worker unrest in societies like France and in the countries of the Anglosphere. The popularity of Herbert Marcuse's *One-Dimensional Man* coincided with a new consciousness among students and workers. This was evidenced in a political militancy that resonated with Marcuse's belief that Western liberal society, under the guise of freedom and democracy, was, in fact, becoming "administered"; where "a free press … censors itself, and [where] free choice is between brands and gadgets." (1964/2002, p. 10). For millions modernity had become repressive and alienating. And by May 1968 the hopes and dreams of the early 1960s counterculture began to generate, if only for a while, a radicalism in French universities and factories.

The turmoil in France was part of a wider political awakening across the so-called New Left. This was a broad association of collectivist organisations, unions, movements and parties that tried to develop forms of socialism and social democracy that constituted an explicit alternative to the politics of the manifestly (to many) un-socialist and unfree regimes of the Soviet bloc (Hall, 2010, pp. 177–197). Issues of culture and ideology began to break free from reductive questions based upon solely economic concerns. Individual freedom, civil rights, feminism, nuclear disarmament and decolonialisation were questions that had been simmering throughout the decade in many developed and developing societies. Major economies like Germany, Italy, Britain and the United States experienced growing social unrest. In the United States, especially, the war in Vietnam served as a lightning rod for the many streams of left-wing dissent. Newspaper media, television news and the expanded role for journalists who worked across both print and television acted as an outlet for the "disparate antiwar and counterculture viewpoints [and so] aided in the organisation of a broad-based and decentralised antiwar coalition" (Tischler, 1990, p. 27). This is not to claim that institutional mass media like the *Washington Post* or CBS television, or individual campaigning journalists, actually *led* the antiwar movement. Indeed, as *Time* magazine correspondent Stanley Karnow suggests in his magisterial book *Vietnam: A History*, it was the other way around, with local and grassroots movements taking the lead. Quoting Gus Wilson, mayor of Bardstown, Kentucky, on the departure of local national guard units to Vietnam in 1968, Karnow illustrates the general mood of disenchantment:

> We believed that the first thing that you did for your country was to defend it. You didn't question that. But I think we realised as we went along – maybe later than we should have – that the government was pulling a bit of a flimflam. We weren't getting the truth. The Vietnam war was being misrepresented to the people – the way it was conducted, its ultimate purpose.
>
> (1997, p. 26)

This rising suspicion of government "flimflam" paralleled claims of a politically supine mass media, including television. Writing of his experiences of the time, Stuart Hall remembered that the "New Left" got little, if any, support or sympathy from the media: "With the expansion of the 'new journalism' and the rise of commercial television, society seemed bewitched by images of itself in motion, reflecting off its shiny consumer surfaces" (2010, p. 187).

Nonetheless, many were becoming revolted as opposed to "bewitched" by much that postwar society had to offer, not least from provenly mendacious U.S. administrations regarding the "conduct" and the "purpose" of the war in Vietnam. Much of the "truth" of the conflict in Southeast Asia would emerge sensationally in 1971 with the reporting by the *New York Times* of the so-called Pentagon Papers, which revealed systemic government secrecy and deception—misinformation fed to the media and the people—going all the way back to 1960. But other truths had begun to appear before the Pentagon Papers *exposé*. Independently, students in the United States had begun demonstrating against the war in Vietnam as early as 1963—at a time when there were still only military advisers there. The first "substantial demonstration" occurred in October of that year, involving students at the University of Wisconsin against the U.S. support for the corrupt and repressive Diem regime in South Vietnam. The innovation of the teach-in became popular, where faculty and students would gather to discuss methods of practical political action. The first began at the University of Michigan in 1965 and spread across the country. A famous teach-in occurred at the University of California at Berkeley during May 1965, and, in October, after speeches and discussions, 15,000 students marched to the Oakland Army Terminal, a facility from where materiel, supplies and men were regularly transported to Vietnam (PBS, 2023).

There was another important dimension to the national groundswell, one relatively overlooked yet one that brought together elements of a more positive "new journalism" with a very different storytelling narrative. It helped bring leading elements of mainstream print and television news into opposition to the war by means of an original and dynamic fusion of old "graphosphere" and new electronic-digital "videosphere" narratives. This development constituted a turning point in media history. It marked the beginning of the end of the dominance by print culture and print capitalism—and it would signal the terminal decline of the analog print journalism that had been a part of Enlightenment-based modernity since the 18th century.

This story begins with a fascinating essay by Barbara L. Tischler on the underground anti-war newspapers produced by disaffected veterans and still-serving soldiers who had been in Vietnam. They constituted a significant movement that:

> began to expound a broad protest agenda … as soldiers began to see themselves as occupying the front ranks of a multi-faceted struggle against American imperialism abroad and injustice at home.
>
> (1990, p. 20)

Tischler tells us that this "broad protest agenda" was the blossoming of "hundreds of underground or alternative publications produced by individuals, college groups, and organisations that identified with the Left" (p. 24). This para-journalism, something that erupted spontaneously, was a movement that gave meaning and solidarity to many thousands of isolated and frustrated soldiers who otherwise would have remained thwarted and ineffectual. "GI journalists" also reached out to more organised allies, such the GI Alliance, GIs United Against the War in Indochina, Movement for a Democratic Military, the United States Servicemen's Fund and Vietnam Veterans Against the War. Military-based groupings also forged links with civil society, like the revolutionary anti-war groups that sprung up, and they were tapped for theoretical guidance and production methods. Actual content, however, the writing that filled the pages of these newspapers, was non-standard and was commissioned from young working-class draftees (after 1969) based on "you write it, we'll print it" (p. 24). The writing *style* is a significant and underappreciated point that Tischler makes, observing that "many of the GI papers opted for the direct, often unedited but authentic, voice of the soldier". Spelling and grammar were often not corrected but were left to preserve their "originality" and "integrity" (p. 24). Tischler:

> The idea that GI antiwar papers presented the views of their readers as they were, without censorship, modification, or the veneer of professional editing or typesetting was an article of faith with many editorial staffs that regarded form as subordinate to content.
>
> (p. 24)

Given that the GIs were the ones doing the fighting and dying, what they had to say about the nature and context of the war, their content was, almost literally, explosive. It had a legitimacy and "truth" that the polished phrases of the professional journalist, even ones reporting from the frontline, could not convey with the same authority. The fact that they could write, however inarticulately, about issues of class and race within the military, about the incompetence of the "brass", and, after 1969, write directly to draftees about fundamental questions like being "caught in the contradiction of having to fight a professional soldier's war without the commitment of the long-term fighter" (p. 27) was galvanising. In 1970, Murray Polner, writing for *Columbia Journalism Review*, conducted a survey of some of the hundreds of publications that formed the "underground GI press" and reprints a typical letter from Vietnam in a GI publication titled, appropriately enough, *Rough Draft,* declaring that: "I tell you in all honesty that out of the 100-plus men here at HQ, you will not find one man who would state we are right in being here" (Polner, 1970, p. 55). In their writing, GI journalists reflected a seriously disillusioned and semi-rebellious military—a potentially catastrophic development for the U.S. government. Returning soldiers burned their draft cards, threw away their medals in public displays of disgust, demonstrated with students and left-wing movements and continued to write "in all honesty" in their DIY outlets to anyone who would read it. The many GI antiwar publications, as Tischler and Polner make clear, and befitting trained soldiers, were adepts of organisation amongst themselves. Individual papers printed lists of other GI anti-war publications, friendly coffeehouses and various drop-in and counselling centres where veterans could meet and exchange news and views about the war and how to promote opposition to it through *their* knowledge and the reality it corresponded to.

The GI journalists looked outwards, too, towards their professional kin in the media for help and advice. In a GI publication satirically titled *Fun, Travel, Adventure (Fort Knox)*, a Vietnam returnee pleaded with readers by way of a letter: "Isn't there one newspaper in this country that cares enough about us to haunt the stockades and report what really goes on?" (Polner, 1970, p. 55). But mainstream media—the press and television—did care, or at least cared enough professionally to take an interest in what going on. Tischler again: "GI newspapers emerged in part to fill a gap in the mainstream press coverage of news that GIs though (sic) was important" (1990, p. 23). Once they had filled it, it occupied a part of the mosaic that was mass media, civil society and a broad front of left-wing and dissenting thought. And the GI journalists with their hundreds of publications and thousands of activists helped create something like a perfect storm of popular opposition to Vietnam; a new media created and sustained "broad protest agenda" that incorporated much of the frustrations that had grown throughout the 1960s. Vietnam was the most important issue of the era. It roused millions into a different awareness, through new forms of knowledge made possible, as we will see, by a newspaper-television convergence in news gathering and distribution that did something unprecedented in terms of the narrative construction of reality through journalism.

Mainstream media, the Tet Offensive and the release of the "now"

The Tet Offensive has been seen as a strategic turning point in the Vietnam War. Launched by the North Vietnamese Army (NVA) in January 1968, it was a simultaneous offensive against many towns and cities throughout the South, including the capital, Saigon. Defeated militarily, the offensive nonetheless succeeded in at least one of its aims—to destabilise the politics and morale of the South. More importantly, Tet called into serious question the U.S. commitment to the war (Moise, 2017). And as something of a bonus for North Vietnam, the role of U.S. media in its coverage of the war during and after Tet was to be a significant factor in turning public opinion against it and leading eventually to a full military withdrawal in 1975.

In terms of media coverage of the war, which began in the late 1950s, newspaper and television outlets conducted an elaborate *pas de deux* with military authorities over the reporting of the fighting and the political atmosphere surrounding it. Based in hotels in Saigon, correspondents would gather daily for briefings from the military press office, dubbed the "five o'clock follies". They were given a menu list of positive, enthusiastic and often misleading accounts of military operations against the NVA and the Viet Cong guerrilla army. War correspondents would go out on their own, to the front or to areas in the rear, looking for stories that would interest their editors and readership. In the main, however, what they produced was standard reporting, as opposed to opinion or criticism of the government or military. However, accounts of these information sessions show them as increasingly strained affairs. Professional decorum between military and media was eventually fractured by the growth of the so-called credibility gap, a euphemism used by the media to describe the increasingly apparent dishonesty of the military and government in relation to the progress of the war (Karnow, 1997, p. 18). The morale-shattering effect of the Tet Offensive was, in the words of Henry Kissinger, the U.S. secretary of state, a "watershed" moment and something that could not so easily be propagandised or covered up. Things began to look very different for the American public after Tet. And when even supporters of government policy began to question what the fighting and dying was for, then effectively both sides of public opinion had become "horrified and dismayed" by the stories that appeared every day in the morning papers and on nightly television news (Karnow, 1997, p. 18).

Despite this growing pessimism, many senior U.S. soldiers maintained in public that Tet was, for the North Vietnamese, "a resounding tactical failure" (Falk, 1988, p. 398). However, senior political officials, like Kissinger, took a more abstract perspective, and instead they "denounced America's television networks and newspapers, contending that their distortions had turned U.S. opinion against the war" (Karnow, 1997, p. 17). As far as the media process itself went, what occurred was a "watershed" moment, not only for the war, but also for the future of journalism.

The technological *cause* of the convergence of newspapers and television, of print and electronic media, has been largely overlooked in comparison to its more familiar political *consequences*. The fusion occurred through a process of "remediation", where, in the words of David Bolter and Richard Grusin: "one medium [newspaper] is incorporated or represented in another [television]" (1999, p. 45). "The goal is not to replace the earlier forms … but rather to spread the content over as many markets as possible" (p. 89). At bottom, it is business. In the case of newspaper-television remediation, however, the media "functioned in a constant dialectic" with each other (p. 50). How did this work in the case of the reporting of Vietnam?

The travel of the dialectic is traceable. And post-Tet it went something like this: for much of their content, nightly television newsreaders used items from their television reporters in the field. However, they also fed off newspaper reporting from earlier in the day for more content, which they read off the autocue—"Today the *New York Times* reported that…". This was expressed as increasingly frank and critical editorialising coming from national television channels that likely amplified the "horror and dismay" that the newspaper reader may have felt whilst reading the *Times* story earlier in the day. In their turn, newspaper editors consumed the nightly images that television journalists had filmed in the war zone, "hot news stories" that were broadcast by the networks soon after they occurred. These visuals could be renarrativised by print journalists and editors to feature as critical commentary for the following day's morning editions.

The direction of the dialectic was evidenced when Walter Cronkite, "the nation's most reliable journalistic personality", underwent an on-screen Damascene conversion regarding the war. Up until Tet, Cronkite the newsreader had been "balanced, nearly bland" in his views about the war. On 27 February 1968, a month after Tet had begun, and just returned from Saigon, Cronkite gave his unequivocal live-to-air judgement, declaring that he was: "more certain than ever that the bloody experience of Vietnam is to end a stalemate" (Karnow, 1997, p. 561). His conversion was late, however. Karnow writes of this moment, which had "shocked and depressed" a watching President Lyndon Johnson: "Cronkite" he observes, "like all other journalists, was lagging behind the American public—reflecting rather than shaping its attitudes" (Karnow, 1997, p. 561).

We see the reverse direction of the dialectic reflected in a historic example of newspapers feeding off television, when Kim Phuc Phan Thi, a nine-year-old village girl from Trang Bang in South Vietnam was filmed on 8 June 1972 running naked and burning from a U.S. Air Force–delivered napalm bomb that had exploded nearby. This highly distressing footage was screened across all the U.S. networks and was hours later published as a front-page graphic image in newspapers all around the world, this time with little commentary or editorialising necessary beyond the barest facts. Such was the extent of transformed public opinion—that the photographs spoke for themselves.

The newspaper-television dialectic thus created a new and dynamic narrative form, where the broadcast words of a Cronkite could mix with film images of a burning girl or a burning village or a summary execution of a suspected guerrilla with blood spurting from a hole in his right temple. These and many other examples helped motivate individuals to take to the streets to protest, and there to be filmed by television crews and reported by newspapers from which more content was created for the evening bulletins and morning editions and for the cycle to repeat itself. As more was known then more was shown in an increasingly freewheeling cycle of print and television remediation that served mainly to "disenchant the American people" (Karnow, 1997, p. 502).

As suggested earlier, the transformation of the narrative form that created the media stories in the late stages of the Vietnam conflict was fundamental but is something that has been almost completely overlooked. Some historical-theoretical context can help to further clarify the process.

In 1946, only twenty or so years before the height of the Vietnam War reporting, John Hersey wrote perhaps the original "new journalism" essay, titled "Hiroshima", about the dropping of an atomic bomb on that Japanese city in August of the year before. As a 31,000-word essay, it occupied the entire edition of the *New Yorker* magazine. It was soon afterwards published as a book and has sold millions of copies ever since. As a precursor of Truman

Capote's *In Cold Blood*, Hersey's essay was a classical narrative textual form, but with fictional elements woven through for poignant effect. It was an old literary technique in a new journalistic arrangement where fiction and non-fiction combine for emotional and literary force in a still-familiar print culture mode. Nevertheless, selling millions of copies on such an important subject does not make for the rise of a social movement or necessarily change public opinion in a way that leads to public policy change. No more bombs were dropped on civilians after Hiroshima and Nagasaki, which is clearly positive, but production and research in atomic and nuclear weapons continued uninterrupted from the 1950s until today. Nuclear testing was halted in 1992 but supercomputers allow physicists and engineers to use visualisation technology to virtually test the effects of blast waves and radiation fallout. And it hardly needs to be stated that gruesome killings (or the execution of their perpetrators) did not stop or even decline in the United States after the publication of Capote's book.

Hersey and Capote's efforts to take journalism into a higher, more literary level, where readers could almost subjectively "experience" the aftermath of an atomic bomb detonation or the details around the murder of a family in an isolated farmhouse, failed—at least at the level of classical journalism and its primary public sphere role. The essay and books were print culture narrative reading. These were authored and controlled in the form in which "word follows word from beginning to end" and in a way that "the reader follows or is supposed to follow", as Derrida put it, shaping the reading experience in a familiarly modern way, the way since the beginnings of the novel form. The millions of buyers of *Hiroshima* and in *Cold Blood* knew how it would end before they bought it. And the ends, once printed, can never change, nor can they be open to change. And those readers, to varying levels of immersion, gave themselves over to the vatic power of the words on the pages and felt empathy, horror, outrage, sympathy and a host of other emotions based upon their personality predispositions and how deeply and closely they engaged with the texts. But the engagement was always an abstract one. A singular process of "silent scanning" as Eisenstein put it, of engaging with the world in the way the writing presents it; a world of abstracted events that in their representation by means of words on paper serve principally to "*dis-engage knowledge* from the arena where human beings struggle with each other" (Ong, 1992, p. 43), which is the actual material world lived in by the reader. Furthermore, such disengagement of knowledge from its object renders "truth" more abstract, something outside the subjective realm where the reader physically exists when not reading. It is experience set in a private as opposed to a public sphere. This is literature, not journalism.

The classical narrative form that Christain Metz (2000, p. 89) tells us "suppresses the now or the here" is an important observation that is revealing if extended for our purposes. In literature, narrative does what it did for Hersey and Capote in their failed attempts to transform journalism. It suppresses the experiential "now" of the reader, the lived presence that reading cognitively extricates one from. However, the remediation of print culture with electronic broadcasting began, in our Vietnam example, to restructure the narrative message. Its linearity became disordered. News begins to move into a dynamic cycle, of constant disordering and reordering of the stories being told. There is no beginning, climax or end to them. This was "rolling" news, to use the industry parlance, and the engagement of the reader or consumer "rolled" with it. The fundamental insight is that the active blend of print and television had the effect of lifting the suppressive force of printed words that sublimated the present time of the reader. The fusion of print, voice and imagery engages the consumer in a new way. This is engagement on a time-space compression basis, where events that occurred only hours ago in a faraway country are beamed into the private sphere of the home in full colour and with narration from journalists on the spot. This is slow by today's technical standards, but, in the closing phase of the Vietnam War, such dramatic and vivid content seemed fresh and alive and vitally current. And with a great deal of freedom to roam with a television crew, and looking for stories that would fit with the turning of opinion on the war, remediated journalists could interview and film frontline soldiers taking drugs, burning villages with Zippo lighters or napalm, mistreating and killing prisoners and civilians or being openly critical of their government and superiors in the military.

The new narratives of the newspaper-television dialectic meant that an ideologically charged story entered the homes of Americans and the national public sphere. Stories of the war expanded out of homes onto streets, where at demonstrations, workplaces, universities and elsewhere, a technologically advanced form of news and stories was able to take possession of the consciousness of individuals as never before—or not since the development of writing. For many activists and distressed citizens, the war had come to them via a print media amplified and rendered "vivid and dramatic" by television (Mitchell, 1984, p. 45). This was an often-troubling part of an everyday postmodernity that they were beginning to experience. As Brock J. Vaughan put it:

> American citizens saw others expressing their feelings publicly in city streets, demanding any U.S. involvement in Vietnam to be stopped. Television had the power to bring these scenes to viewers on a massive scale than any other medium at the time. Televised stories of the anti-war movement and the events transpiring in Vietnam were often interlinked, falling in the same news segments which ultimately … blurred the distinction between the battlefield and the home front.
>
> (2020, p. 7)

Vaughan and others like Paul Joseph accentuate the power of television. And not for nothing the Vietnam war has been called the first "television war".

Joseph: "Television reduced the space between the battlefield and the viewer. When the media showed the intensity and the chaos of the war with relatively little mediation, it helped turn people against the war" (2017). This is a partly accurate assessment, but newspapers were still a useful part of what was a new media formation. An "old" media was being remediated by the new, to become something else, a hybrid media with a reader effect that was expressed as a different perceptual engagement with the world. The "message" of this evolved news media, to channel Marshal McLuhan once more, is that the narrative message had been transformed and the suppressed "now" of print culture was now opened up. This fusion, with its unstable narrative form was, we see in hindsight, a precursor to digitality, to the Internet and social media. In the late 1960s and going on into the early years of the 1970s, the Vietnam media experience opened up a window of possibility for a different kind of public sphere; one more democratic and reflective of the sentiments and political consciousness of an engaged and exponentially more "mass" population. Why this would not eventuate, and what this meant for journalism, we will consider shortly. For now, we continue with the conjectural development of how print journalism had reached its apogee and then the decline of classical-modern influence during these few years of remediation and transition.

It was John Hersey himself who prefigured the "end of the newspaper" trope that has become established today. As R. Z. Sheppard wrote in *Time* magazine in 1985:

> After publication of *Hiroshima*, Hersey noted that "the important 'flashes' and 'bulletins' are already forgotten by the time yesterday morning's paper is used to line the trash can. The things we remember are emotions and impressions and illusions and images and characters: the elements of fiction".
>
> (n.p.n)

The "flashes" and "bulletins" of Hersey's 1940s had become the satellite and networked television of McLuhan's 1960s "global village"; and they, along with newspapers, left rather more than dreamlike "impressions and illusions". They were able, at least in nascent form, to become part of the *lived mediated present*. This was a developing "mediascape", as Arjun Appadurai would later phrase it, an electronic- and digital-created context where newspapers and television were able to form part of the new "building blocks of … imagined worlds" (1990, p. 33) that were the ontological extensions of the modern "imagined communities" of Anderson's "print capitalism" or Eisenstein's "print culture". This was a mediascape that was no longer so abstract and controlled by means of print but something potentially more diverse and able to produce "multiple worlds" (ibid). In the late 1960s, and with political and social turmoil beginning to become ingrained within Western culture,

Vietnam was a glowering spectre in the "multiple worlds" that formed the lived present of millions who experienced it, virtually or physically. And the content was instrumental in channelling a growing opposition to the war to the point of political crisis for the U.S. administration. This was stated in personal terms by President Johnson, who, at the end of March 1968, almost three months after the beginning of the Tet Offensive, announced that he would not run for reelection that year, believing privately that the war had made him deeply unpopular with U.S. citizens. The newspaper-television nexus that had catalysed around the drama of the Tet Offensive was accelerant for an already "burning fuse of dissent" (Karnow, 1997, p. 557) that changed print forever.

Expressive of the effect of the newspaper-television remediation and the breakdown of the classical print narrative structure was an inconspicuous line buried in an obscure document titled "The First Television War" published in the *Encyclopedia of American Foreign Relations*. The unnamed author states that the power of television: "came from what NBC News executive Reuven Frank said television journalism did best, which was the *transmission of experience*" (EAFR, 2023) (my emphasis). This form of "experience" was, arguably, an early form of VR immersivity, where a dialectic between the technologies of print and television engages the consumer with a new narrative power in a way not previously possible. This development came freighted with extraordinary potentiality and would lead to the forms and processes of technological communication that would, with the Internet and social media, as Régis Debray wrote, "enable thought to have social existence" (2007, p. 5) within a new cognitive mediascape with its own "multiple worlds". The transmission of experience—in this early innovation—is given social existence in the minds of those engaged with the newspaper-television cycle in part through its capacity to "create the physical conditions … through the means of communication" for "the annihilation of space by time" (Marx, 1973, p. 449). In other words, communication media tends to *shrink* the world in our perception and *speed up* our experience of it—bringing us cognitively, representationally and temporally closer to everything and everything closer to us. The newspaper-television remediation thus contributed positively to the ending of an imperialist war and would earn Pulitzer Prizes for many journalists and photographers who reported on it. It would also, and just as famously, earn Pulitzer Prizes for the journalists who would work on the Watergate scandal a few years later, an investigation that would help bring down President Johnson's successor in the White House and change the relationship between the political executive and the media—and not necessarily in a positive way for the media (Balz, 2022). We see in retrospect that this period was classical-modern journalism's Indian summer in respect of "speaking truth to power" and contributing positively to a dynamic public sphere. Wider technological and economic processes were already well underway at this time, and these would lead eventually to the digital age that heralded the protracted and still not fully understood existential crises that afflict the craft and profession of journalism today.

As the technological and ideological forces that would create a global marketplace gathered pace during the 1970s, in the narrower world of state and fourth estate relations in the United States, the dangerous new potency of the newspaper-television remediation was not lost in military and policy circles. In the United States and elsewhere, the post-Vietnam reckoning of "what went wrong" would serve to constrain journalistic freedom in conflict zones.

After the U.S. withdrawal from Vietnam in 1975, the idea of the press as being the "agents of defeat" (Hammond, 1989, p. 312) was something that exercised the minds of many politicians and military officials. The influential conservative journalist Robert Elegant, someone with long experience of reporting in Vietnam, wrote in an August 1981 edition of *Encounter* magazine:

> The Western press appears either unaware of the direct connection between cause (its reporting) and effect (the Western defeat in Viet Nam), or strangely reluctant to proclaim that the pen and the camera proved decisively mightier than the bayonet and ultra-modern weapons.

Closer to the action in at least one respect was Major Michael C. Mitchell of the U.S. Marine Corps, who concurred. Writing in 1984 for the *Naval War College Review*, he drew on contemporaneous studies of the media and measured them against the Television Code of the National Association of Broadcasters that legally obliges television companies that their news reporting be "factual, fair, and without bias" (Mitchell, 1984, p. 44). Mitchell cites what he called the "most damning" of the various reports by the controversial political theorist Ernest Lefever, who studied the CBS-TV news content between 1972 and 1973 (he considered CBS as typical of the TV industry at large) and determined that:

> CBS Evening News was seriously deficient in presenting a fair, full and meaningful picture of national security developments [in Vietnam].

Mitchell takes this and more of Lefever's research at face value. Moreover, he believes that the *technology of television* itself constituted a good part of the problem. And betraying a somewhat one-dimensional perspective on the medium, he writes that "television is above all else an entertainment industry", and:

> In its efforts to attract and maintain audiences, therefore, television has often sought to broadcast news events more for their dramatic value than for their informational content.
>
> (p. 50)

However, the Marine changes from ideologue to diplomat in his summation, where he argues, presciently as it turns out, for a kind of future partnership between the military and the "media" (not just television):

> The military must not lose sight of the fact that its foremost responsibility is to prosecute wars. [...] What both the military and media need to do is to learn each other's particular responsibilities and limitations, to accept each other as imperfect occupiers of the battlefield, each having a particular mission to fulfill, and then to establish mutually agreeable working compromises that allow them both to meet their objectives.
>
> (p. 51)

We now know what "responsibilities and limitations" would mean for journalists in war zones: It meant "embedding", a process where journalists are controlled by military minders in their accreditation, movements and access to information. Embedding was in fact something pioneered operationally by the British government in the 1982 Falklands war where, as BBC journalist Brian Hanrahan wrote, it was an unequal "pact with the devil" where journalists had no choice whether to participate or not (Wyatt, 2012). Its "success" in the Falklands meant that it became a template for the 21st-century U.S. wars in Iraq and Afghanistan, where embedding and hence public perceptions of the conflict would by shaped by overriding political and military exigencies. Embedding dealt a blow to the professionalism and ethics in what Tom Paine in *The Rights of Man* called the journalist's "the dignity of freedom" to point out where "mystery and secrecy on one side is opposed to candour and openness on the other" (2018, p. 61).

The curbing of such "dignity of freedom" was rationalised in a 2003 U.S. Defence Department memorandum, accessed via a Freedom of Information Act request in 2006. The context of journalistic freedom had changed since Vietnam, but the central importance of control over *the story*, had not. The memorandum was addressed to the very highest levels of government, and it read, in part:

> MEDIA COVERAGE OF ANY FUTURE OPERATION WILL, TO A LARGE EXTENT, SHAPE PUBLIC PERCEPTION OF THE NATIONAL SECURITY ENVIRONMENT NOW AND IN THE YEARS AHEAD. [...] OUR ULTIMATE STRATEGIC SUCCESS IN BRINGING PEACE AND SECURITY TO THIS REGION WILL COME IN OUR LONG-TERM COMMITMENT TO SUPPORTING OUR DEMOCRATIC IDEALS. ***WE NEED TO TELL THE FACTUAL STORY*** - GOOD OR BAD - BEFORE OTHERS SEED THE MEDIA WITH DISINFORMATION AND DISTORTIONS, AS THEY MOST CERTAINLY WILL CONTINUE TO DO. OUR PEOPLE IN THE

> FIELD NEED TO TELL *OUR STORY* - **ONLY COMMANDERS CAN ENSURE THE MEDIA GET TO THE STORY ALONGSIDE THE TROOPS**. WE MUST ORGANIZE FOR AND FACILITATE ACCESS OF NATIONAL AND INTERNATIONAL MEDIA TO OUR FORCES, INCLUDING THOSE FORCES ENGAGED IN GROUND OPERATIONS, WITH THE GOAL OF DOING SO RIGHT FROM THE START. TO ACCOMPLISH THIS, WE WILL EMBED MEDIA WITH OUR UNITS. THESE EMBEDDED MEDIA WILL LIVE, WORK AND TRAVEL AS PART OF THE UNITS WITH WHICH THEY ARE EMBEDDED TO FACILITATE MAXIMUM, IN-DEPTH COVERAGE OF U.S. FORCES IN COMBAT AND RELATED OPERATIONS. COMMANDERS AND PUBLIC AFFAIRS OFFICERS MUST WORK TOGETHER TO BALANCE THE NEED FOR MEDIA ACCESS WITH THE NEED FOR OPERATIONAL SECURITY.
>
> (US Department of Defense, 2006)

A fundamental lesson learned by many governments post-Vietnam was that in a rapidly expanding communication-rich environment of print, television and the coming age of digital, journalists and journalism could no longer continue as before. Paine's "dignity of freedom", such as it ever really existed anyway, was increasingly seen by governments as a luxury tolerated sometimes, and a national security threat at most other times. And so, in the decades after the 1970s, journalists in conflict zones became more controlled, with governments seeking to "telling our story" as they understood (or wished) it to be. Notwithstanding the seriousness of this assault on the freedom of the press, after a period of public and journalistic uneasiness over the ethics of embedding, the issue soon disappeared. And with the world changing rapidly as a communicative space, and with media institutions under technological threat from the Internet, governments felt strong enough to concede little, if any, of the general principles of the embedding and restricting process and its muzzling of the media.

Beyond the redacted dramas of the Falklands, Iraq, Afghanistan, Guantanamo Bay Naval Base and elsewhere, the world continued to turn, but at a quicker rate. The postwar social-democratic experiment with planned or semi-planned economies, large and growing welfare states, high taxes and nationalised industries had begun to crumble into economic as well as social crises (see Harvey, 1982; 1989). The turn towards globalisation and a free market, with low taxes and privatisation across the Anglosphere and beyond, is a well-known story that need not detain us here. Less well known as a vital contributing factor to the globalisation process and all it entailed has been the revolution in computing. Computation had been a slow-burning technology for decades, confined mainly to the military and to large bureaucratic and information-heavy sectors like banking, finance and insurance. The 1970s, a hinge decade in so many ways, was when this began to change. Transformation in the economy towards globalisation, automation and rationalisation were technology driven (see Lash & Urry, 1987) and spurred investments into computer based "solutions" of every kind. As Daniel Bell argued in his *The Coming of Post-Industrial Society* (1973) the developed world was leading the way to the creation of a post-industrial society, where information and knowledge, instead of the machines of heavy industry, would be the new main generators of value. This was information and knowledge that was optimally utilised through rationalisation and organisation, via what he quaintly termed the "codification of theoretical knowledge"—meaning computerisation (Bell, 1973, p. 576). It was during the early part of the 1980s that for the first time more dollar investment went into computer and related high-technology equipment than went into traditional labour-intensive machinery in the United States (Kolko, 1988, p. 61). Capitalism's insatiable need to create value through "efficient" means of production meant that a neoliberal information age was becoming an unstoppable reality.

Recall the philosophical debates on the nature of analog and digital at the Macy Conference of 1950 that we considered previously, when even in the context of the Cold War, at least some intellectual thought was given to what powerful computer systems meant for society beyond their instrumental use. There were very few philosophical questions being asked this time as computerisation was now dubbed a progressive "revolution" and was tirelessly promoted and embraced by all kinds of boosters, industrialists, politicians and, increasingly, consumers themselves. Computers were touted, in the words of Theodore Roszak, as a universal panacea, as a "solution in search of a problem" (1986, p. 51). Like globalisation, the story of the rise of the Internet and social media is well known. But much of the common history is one of general positivity in business and in the cultural lives of people. The success stories of Silicon Valley corporations are seen as analogous to the successes of post-industrialism and those economies and societies that embraced market-based globalisation. With the Western economies in the lead, cheap or free communication through networks of data would, we were told ceaselessly, create a world that would be less hierarchical, where everyone could be an author or a citizen journalist or a participant in the electronic town hall. Journalism itself, in its increasingly outmoded industry of daily printed news and journalists belonging to unions with codes of ethics and professional standards, had to get with the program. But the newspaper industry was never fast enough, or journalists were never embracing of change enough, and so crises set in early as computerisation spread unabated after the defeat of the print unions at Wapping in 1986.

Over the years, various journalist-academics have identified and critiqued this transformation, and the literature offers an often-perceptive political economy analysis of the problems of the sector and the profession (e.g.,

McChesney, 2013). However, the rolling crises for journalism were always more than political and economic. The political and economic reaches deep down into the anthropologic, into what it means to be human, and our relationship with technology. It has also been considered in this writing that we are experiencing a crisis of *communication*, and a crisis more particularly of *writing and storytelling*. In other words, a crisis of the very basis of literacy and the effects of writing—the very foundations upon which journalism was conceived and founded in the 17th century. So the crisis is philosophical as it is political-economic. But the philosophical or ethical has rarely been an aspect of the inspirations of Silicon Valley or capitalism more broadly. But nothing occurs in a vacuum, and, as early as the 1970s, at the embryonic phase of popular computerisation, the new technology was perceived by some as a distinct threat to ideas of truth, of knowledge and how we come to these epistemes and communicate these in our cultures and societies. One of these was Jean François Lyotard, and his *The Postmodern Condition: A Report on Knowledge*. The book is well known in certain circles, and a notable idea from it is that the "postmodern condition" in the title of the book could be understood as a "incredulity" towards the overarching stories that we tell ourselves, which underpin our cultures and orient us within the world (1979, p. xxiv).

Lyotard's perception of a growing philosophical and cultural doubt about metanarratives are the subject of the next chapter. There we look at how and why the stories we wrote and told ourselves, generation after generation, began to make less sense to us, didn't seem to fit anymore. This will give us another relatively underappreciated perspective on the predicament of the modern journalist as writer and communicator and will show how the new world of networked computation makes for an impossible context for the journalist to carry on in the way they had and with the tools they had since the time of Voltaire.

5 Digital discontinuity

Writing, narrative and the fracturing of the journalist's story

Late modernity and the sovereignty of numbers over words

The forms and processes of "communication" that we refer to here is communication in its *modern* forms and processes: the *print culture* communication that was in no small measure cause and consequence of modernity itself—and what it entailed as an economic, philosophical, political and cultural phenomena. And journalism, as a craft and a profession, was at the heart of this modernity. Journalistic communication through the production of its own narratives is what made the fourth estate, the public sphere and the mass media. These were the prominent realms of print-based interaction that informed and shaped the democratic struggles of the modern age. Moreover, the communication between capital and labour, ideologies and political parties, government institutions and businesses, all depended upon the same *forms of print knowledge* being produced and shared between the different stakeholders. And it was the broadly accepted *legitimacy* of these narratives that was able to bestow upon the "institutions of knowledge" (Lyotard, 1979, p. 17) like the sciences, the arts and politics, a *relative* stability and "internal equilibrium" (Lyotard, 1979, p. 7) such that modernity could develop into the dominant form that would, by the post-1945 era, incorporate much of the world.

But this equilibrium was veering towards implosion. Marx and Engels's characterisation of capitalist dynamism as "all that is solid melts into air, all that is holy is profaned" (1976, p. 39) depicted an always accelerating pace of change, meaning that the "institutions of knowledge" were never as stable, timeless and progressive as many imagined them to be. Indeed, *nothing* under capitalism can be said to be constant apart from its relations of exploitation in search of profitability (Wark, 2021, pp. 39–101). Classical Marxism imagined that this unsteady dynamism would herald the ultimate crisis between the classes, and communism would result. It hasn't. A liberal-capitalist political strain within modernity has long been dominant. And within this *longue durée*, from the late 19th century onwards, increasingly powerful institutions in business and in politics, with Western Europe and North America foremost, oversaw liberal capitalism's transformative energy as expressing, for many, almost the natural order of things. A market-based capitalism that harnessed

DOI: 10.4324/9781003054207-6

and encouraged science and literacy was the supposed impulse that propelled the upward curve of a common human progress. Modernity was our predestination, and, under the arc of its metanarratives, it was where journalism was born.

However, all this modernising, by its very nature, was characterised by a growing complexity. This is a problem for the efficient management of the economic system especially, the realm that creates productive technologies. Capitalism as the driver of modernity thus creates a paradox for itself in relation to complexity. On the one hand, complexity is the inevitable outcome of a system based on constant innovation and growth. This requires rational managerial systems of information and knowledge to be constantly applied so as to avoid chaos, ensure predictability and create the optimum conditions for further rounds of innovation and growth. On the other hand, these additional information and knowledge systems must themselves be necessarily more complex so as to manage the growing complexity of capitalism. Consider Neil Postman's *Technopoly: The Surrender of Culture to Technology* in 1992:

> Technology increases the available supply of information. As the supply is increased, control mechanisms are strained. Additional control mechanisms are needed to cope with the new information. When additional control mechanisms are themselves technical, they in turn further increase the supply of information.
>
> (p. 73)

Following McLuhan and Ong, Postman argued in his *Amusing Ourselves to Death* (1985) that "public discourse" was being transformed negatively by the new electronic-digital media. He argued that the "print-based epistemology" of modernity in the United States, "the most print-oriented culture to have ever existed", was being destabilised by television and the personal computing revolution, which together formed a techno-logic that was "creating new kinds of truth-telling" (p. 33). The monopoly that print had over truth was being weakened and undermined by the powerful combination of television and computers. Indeed, print was further losing its illustrious position, symbolised in the 1982 founding of *USA Today*, which, according to Postman, was when newspapers began more fully to resemble the entertainment-television format (p. 96). The effect of this new media engagement was that "the public is being amused into indifference" (p. 95).

At a more philosophical level, Postman believed computers represented a particularly potent expression of an *enchantment with numbers* that runs deep in Western culture. It is a fascination and belief that only now, via the latest advances in computer technology, was able to penetrate human consciousness—in the way that print once did—to express a "truth" of its own. As Postman sees it, new technology and computing was imposing an ever more fundamental "sovereignty of numbers" (p. 30) into modern culture and economy. What this means in practical terms is that in an increasingly complex capitalist reality, the "truth" of numbers means that everything *can and should* be measured so to be communicated as a value. And so from human IQ to GDP, and from genome sequencing to financial markets, numbers give the measure and, hence, an inherent market value to everything and anything. Postman's media-related point was that if a message can be communicated by means of print or television or the new power of the computer, then it creates a value and therefore communicates a new truth of its own. The problem, as Postman saw it, was that "as print wanes, the content of politics, religion, education, and anything else that comprises public business must change and be recast" (p. 19) to reflect the logic and affordances of the new media form.

"Noise" is the sound of analog

The connections between narrative and communication are explored a little more at this juncture. In particular, we consider an influential concept of technical "communication" developed by Claude Shannon that has influenced the structure and application of computer systems. This short discussion will set the scene for the next section that traces the effect of digital communication upon the narratives that previously acted as moorings that held modernity more or less in place, and functioning as the more or less trusted vectors through which journalists reported the world to us in printed form.

Shannon's essay, *The Mathematical Theory of Communication,* was published in 1948 and would become the standard model for communication and information theory and would form the technical standard that underpins information systems today. It's notable that Shannon trained as a mathematician and computer scientist and that his twenty-four-page essay was conceived and articulated exclusively within its rigid disciplinary boundaries. For him, communication is understood not according to any humanist or philosophical standard, but in *cybernetic* terms, as stochastic patterns of information and "noise" to be coded and decoded in any number of configurations by the communicative apparatus itself. The central goal that the model seeks to achieve is a *maximum precision* in the sending of a message (the coding) to its receipt (the decoding) via the channel (the medium). Getting in the way of a perfect cybernetic exchange in these steps is what Shannon calls "noise" like signal distortion or, in more human terms, any perceived interference that causes the message to be less than fully understood. The reduction of "noise" by means of improved technical systems for coding and decoding (all seen as technical-mathematical problems) is the overarching aim towards an ultimately "noiseless" channel communication of information (Shannon, 1948, pp. 3–18).

The title of Shannon's essay points to a major objection to the model as being of universal applicability. Based entirely on mathematics, it implicitly treats the world and humans as abstractions, the "truth" of which are best understood by number. It takes no account of humans as flawed and diverse subjective beings who actually create the codes, the decodes and the media that carry them. As a hyper-rationalised perspective on (human) communication, it makes the same mistake that neoliberal economics would make in the 1970s. Here, too, people were viewed essentially as predictable "rational actors" who, if (in theory) having access to complete information in respect of their economic choices, would "naturally" and always seek to maximise benefits to themselves (e.g., Friedman, 1962). It would see the passing of several decades of neoliberal ideological dominance before the psychologist Daniel Kahneman would debunk the presumed hardwiring of a mathematical rationalism in individuals. Kahneman, indeed, would receive a Nobel Prize in 2002 for exposing the assumptions underlying the idea of *homo economicus* and the neoliberal world that would be based on it. People, Kahneman argued, can very often be *irrational*, even when perfect information is available to them. And in his *Thinking, Fast and Slow*, Kahneman makes the eminently rational point that neoliberal economics and its ideal-typical *homo economicus* is, in fact, a political concept of freedom, not economics, and one "closely linked to an ideology in which it is unnecessary and even immoral to protect people against their choices" (2011, p. 347). Actual people are far more complex, in ways that can't be captured easily or accurately by economic modelling. Optimism, negativity, biases, emotion, genes, hormones, "irrational exuberance" are part of our psychological makeup. Such diversity of perception within us and between us means that we tend to choose anchoring narratives (strong stories, fallacious or true) that help us make sense of a world that would otherwise be almost unintelligible. Postman made a similar observation in *Technopoly* about the need for grounding principles of narrative truth in media because: "the world in which we live is very nearly incomprehensible to most of us" (1992, p. 58).

In print culture, the "noise" that computer scientists obsess about as something to be reduced as much as possible in the quest for perfect communication didn't exist. There was only the "silent" engagement with printed texts that Eisenstein saw as the almost metaphysical engagement with reality, one where the words themselves transport us to a mind's eye meeting with what the words represented. More arresting, perhaps, is Hegel's view that "newspapers serve modern man as a substitute for morning prayer," and that reading a newspaper requires a retreat to the "silent privacy, in the lair of the skull" (Anderson, 1983, p. 35). The thus world represented is controlled by the narrative form and the metanarratives that they rest upon. These are relatively secure over time but may change (or are subject to change) with changes in the technologies that create and disseminate them. In the newspaper-television remediation that we saw previously, the suppression of "the now or the here" that print imposes is released by the new engagement. Sound and moving pictures combined to assail the senses. The "silent privacy" of print reading is exposed to an active world in something close to a real-time experience of the "now or the here" (Metz, 2000, p. 89). That "now or the here" of mediated experience was still analog even in its remediated print-electronic form. However, as we saw in the Vietnam example, the long dominance of print was ending. Its traditional journalistic sphere of current affairs, its fourth estate role and its political dimension in the public sphere were fundamentally challenged by the mediating power of television. And television was able to generate engagement akin to a mediated present, bringing the far to the near, inserting a new consciousness of the world—of a kind that print could never match.

End of story?

Early in the debates about postmodernity, Jürgen Habermas worried that the word "modernity" had "lost [its] fixed historical reference" (1981, p. 4) and that the social edifices of modernity itself were coming loose from their two-hundred-year-old foundations. Neoliberalism was then in the ascendance and promoting its ideological mission through the insertion, via computation, of "administrative rationality" (p. 8) across economy, culture and politics. Habermas worried that the economic and cultural attacks on the "incomplete project" of the Enlightenment by "technical progress, capitalist growth and rational administration" (p. 14) could not be easily stopped. And so it proved to be. The intellectual and social structures of modernity disintegrated substantially in the face of a three-decades-long offensive to shrink the size of government and diminish the scope of regulation, marked by the ambition to bring market forces to almost every aspect of life. Neoliberalism would change the world and engender a form of globalisation such that the whole world would, to some degree, fall under the power of a *postmodern* capitalism—one connected by communication networks—whose fundamental logic was oriented towards a value-creating process of commodification that would "monitor, measure and monetize" everything it could, wherever it could (Winseck, 2011, p. 23).

Insofar as the "master-narratives" of Western civilization discourses were concerned, some of this globalisation seemed positive. A cultural and intellectual postmodernity that carried through the tropes of freedom and left liberalism of the late-1960s kind had begun to challenge many of the old Western-centric faiths. The general thrust is conveyed well by Peter Burke in his *A Social History of Knowledge*, where he writes that a new generation of philosophers and cultural theorists began to direct criticism on:

> what is known as the "Grand Narrative" or master narrative, especially the story of the rise of Western Civilization—Renaissance, Reformation, Enlightenment, French and Industrial Revolutions, and so on—on the grounds that it privileges one part of the world and one social group, upper class males.
>
> (2012, p. 80)

Cause and consequence of this new sensibility was what Lyotard called an "incredulity toward metanarratives" (1979: xxiv). The once unassailable Western meanings were suddenly beginning to look distinctly suspect, as misleadingly one-dimensional, and as history written by white, powerful, European men. This scepticism provoked new ways to look at the past, to find records and create alternative stories, or "microhistories" or "histories of the everyday" (Burke, 2012, p. 80). As Burke continues, "A major aim [in these alternative narratives] was to allow the voices of ordinary men and women to be heard and to include in the story of the ways in which they tried to make sense of their world" (p. 80). Much of this research came from archival, literary and cultural studies and was affirmative in that formerly silenced and disparate voices and lives were heard often for the first time. And through this process of intertextuality, or *bricolage*, a re-assembling of the "cracks in the mirror" of modernity was undertaken, and continues today, to create something, if not new, then different and expressive of another truth and alternative reality (Harvey, 1989, p. 359).

Journalists, too, pursued this postmodern trope of recording other narratives and other stories to sometimes inspiring effect. We see examples in the writings of Robert Fisk, and in *Pity the Nation: Lebanon at War*, where the everyday lives of hitherto anonymous individuals from once "orientalised" cultures and places are brought to salience against a backdrop of post-colonial chaos and war; cultures and places where the white, Western master narratives had little purchase and even less relevance for the subjects he brings to life (1990). Other journalists of Fisk's generation like John Pilger, whose *A Secret Country*: *The Hidden Australia* exposed another history of the continent, one starkly at odds with the Europe-derived narratives of "the Lucky Country". Instead, the "scale and consistency of violence inflicted upon their black compatriots" by the white settlers since 1788 were laid out as new and terrible counter-histories (1989, p. 45). The unearthing of lives and voices from below continues today in the work of Ta-Nehisi Coates, to take just one example. In his *Between the World and Me* (2015) Coates uses a mix of classical long-form journalism and autobiography to focus on the underside of American culture, and brings to the surface the contemporary Black experience, which, like that of the Australian First Nations peoples, was othered and silenced by the historical narratives and power of white settler cultures.

This aspect of journalism's troubled postmodernity is rightly celebrated. And it goes beyond books. Today there is a fragile blossoming of a left-liberal culture of journalism and essay writing that deals with history, politics, art, literary criticism and more—much or all of which still derives its narrative writing ethos from its modernist roots. Legacy titles, like the *New York Times*, the *Guardian*, the *Washington Post*, the *Atlantic*, *n+1*, the *New York Review of Books*, the *London Review of Books*, the *New Yorker* and conservative publications like the *Times* and the *Economist* are serious global brands that endure on the back of globalisation. Early and innovative adopters of digital, these outlets have had to restructure themselves *as* global brands, eschewing the narratives of localism and the nationalism and the traditions that had shaped their former identities (Bell, 2020).

Less celebrated, and less well known, is the communications effect of postmodernity: the unforeseen aspects of digital media devices and systems that enabled globalisation to be what it would become. Increasingly freed from government regulation and restriction from the early 1980s onwards, the logic of Silicon Valley would colonise economy, culture and society through the often mandatory use of their digital products. Life is now increasingly lived through virtual representations created by pixelated and mutable words on screens instead of words fixed on printed pages. The rush to market to sell their communication devices meant that the status knowledge, stories and narratives would be subjected to experimental beta-testing of their products by trialling them on vast and mostly unsuspecting populations. What the beta-testing did not pick up, because it was never a concern for the makers, was that the modern conceptions of "truth" contained and legitimised in the analog texts of print capitalism would face their first and only existential crisis. And we were all too busy looking at screens to notice.

The big breakup: narrative, story, truth

Someone who didn't celebrate the arrival of computerisation was the ever-sceptical Lyotard. Thinking about the new technology philosophically as opposed to from a sociological or a political economy perspective, Lyotard got to the nub or the problem early on, and his *The Postmodern Condition* stands the test of time and change. A new category of technology, he reckoned, means that the type, focus, production and dissemination of knowledge will change accordingly. Lyotard's slim volume, more a pamphlet in the style of Tom Paine, was as much of a sensation as a philosophical work could be in the Anglosphere. Its arguments were written for a specific readership—academics and thinkers in continental philosophy, politics, cultural studies and literature studies. Lyotard writes that "the nature of knowledge cannot survive unchanged within this general context of transformation" (1979, p. 4). He specifies: "it is common knowledge that the miniaturisation and commercialisation of machines is already changing the way in which learning is acquired, classified, made available, and exploited" (p. 4). A narrow commercialisation underlined this transformation of knowledge—and thus the "set of prescriptions determining which statements are accepted as 'knowledge' statements" (p. 4). The determining prescriptions or instructions were commodification and value. Lyotard argues that the "computerization of society" (p. 7) was inevitable following the crises of the postwar economic settlement structured around liberal democracy. Drawing conclusions like contemporaries such as Daniel Bell (1973), he saw the world as changing into a post-industrial phase, where science and technological research and the forms of knowledge it produced, would be the "ultimately determining instance" of value creation within postmodern capitalism (p. xiii). Fredric Jameson disagreed with Lyotard's post-industrial thesis and argued instead (in the foreword to Lyotard's book) that the world was still being "industrialised for the first time" (p. xiv). However, we see now that the old-style industrialisation that Jameson referred to was actually being *relocated*—and in more updated and automated forms—to the newly industrialising economies in Asia and eventually to China, where today it drives much of the global economy in terms of the production of material things. In the West, value and profit, most of it flowing up the social scale, would be extracted increasingly from the commodification of knowledge that would create massive economies of service production. Moreover, this new knowledge would be produced to be sold, in the creation of exchange value. And nothing, or nowhere would be off-limits to the logic of a computerisation process functioning to create, commodify and realise knowledge as value. And when Lyotard wrote, at the end of the 1970s, the "grand narratives of [knowledge] legitimation" (p. 51) were already much diminished. A new instrumentalised narrative was now ascendant. It wasn't a grand narrative but a viral one, constituting its own form of legitimation that would occupy the space that the old narratives of modernity generated. "The question now asked" by the postmodern doubters is:

> no longer "Is it true?" but "What use is it?" In the context of the mercantilization of knowledge, more often than not this question is equivalent to: "Is it saleable?" And in the context of power-growth: "Is it efficient"?
>
> (p. 51)

The questioning of truth has become subordinated to commodified knowledge providing its own truths and its own narratives and one legitimised by numbers. Lyotard again: "When it comes to speaking the truth or prescribing justice [the very essence of the journalistic ethos], numbers are meaningless" (p. 52). This means that modern ethical, moral and subjective notions like "prescribing justice" are difficult to communicate via postmodern computer networks. To understand how and why digitality contributes significantly to the breakup of modern forms of communication, we need to return to our primary thesis of our species' analog-evolved constitution as technology to show that digital does not and cannot communicate meaning in a diverse and baroque human way.

-

An understanding of the breakup of the analog world, the world of the journalist since the 18th century, was prefaced, as noted before, on the differences between analog and digital at the 1950 Macy Conference in New York. R.

W. Gerard informed his audience then that analog processes were expressed by "continuity relations" and digital processes by "discontinuity relations" (Gerard, 1953, p. 172). These seemingly obscure differences were lost in their public significance in a world where computers were exotic and cloistered machines. They existed mainly in theory and those who did think about them focused mostly on their practical uses and on the technical problems at hand. This was in a military-industrial complex scenario where scientists, engineers, physicists and others tended to work on problems at the micro level as opposed to blue-sky, philosophical issues.

It would take almost two decades after Macy before research on the social-psychological aspects of digital communication began to emerge. In 1967 Paul Watzlawick (1921–2007), for example, suggested that digital communication at the human level is *disrupted* and exhibits *less fidelity* in the content of messaging from sender to receiver than through analog means. In other words, when communicating digitally, and notwithstanding the engineers' efforts to reduce "noise", miscommunication often occurs. Watzlawick's work empirically underscores the theory of the breakdown of modern narratives and stories and shows that as we increasingly computerise and digitalise our communication, then the more we misunderstand the world—or at the very least we begin to understand the world *differently* through different forms and processes of communication.

Watzlawick was a relatively unusual combination of psychologist and communications theorist. His *The Pragmatics of Human Communication* specifically compares analog and digital forms of human communication. They contend that the "quantizing" or "discrete" logic of digital described by R. W. Gerard in 1953 was unable to dependably replicate human verbal or nonverbal communication. The study begins with an assessment of analog communication:

> What…is analogic communication? The answer is relatively simple: it is virtually all nonverbal communication. This term, however, is deceptive… We hold that the term must comprise posture, gesture, facial expression, voice inflection, the sequence, rhythm, and cadence of the words themselves, and any other nonverbal manifestation of which the organism is capable, as well as the communicational clues unfailingly present in any *context* in which an interaction takes place.
>
> (1967, p. 62)

To communicate analog human actions though writing is difficult, and this is what novelists, poets and writers, including journalists, have struggled with since the beginnings of the modern literary form. But digital communication can hardly begin to cope with accurately transmitting the "unfailingly" noisy messaging of human expression:

> In digital computers both data and instructions are processed in the form of numbers so that often … there is only an arbitrary correspondence between the particular piece of information and its digital expression.
>
> (pp. 41–42)

Where communication has a "content and relationship aspect", and where "relationship is the central issue in communication", then "digital language is almost meaningless" (1967, pp. 44–45). This is quite a finding. What digital communication lacks is an "adequate vocabulary" (p. 66) to reflect the infinite possibilities of human relationships (p. 47). And so: "Not only can there be no translation from the digital into the analogic mode without great loss of information … but the opposite is extraordinarily difficult" (p. 47). The philosopher Leonard Hawes takes up this work in his book on political conflict in which he emphasises that in human communication it is impossible to *not* communicate; we always communicate something. But a message cannot be translated between the analog and the digital without gaps, voids and potential miscommunication. Digital communication, he writes, lacks "an adequate vocabulary for qualities and shading of relationships' (2015, p. 164).

The philosopher of language, John Searle, shared this perspective on the lack of fidelity in the digital communication of analog speech and writing. In 1980 he argued that the essential difference between *syntax* and *semantics* means that AI will be functionally incapable of consciousness or intelligence as humanly understood. And this has implications for written communication. The syntactic transmission of "facts" are what computers are good at. But his does not mean that the reader of syntactically correct "facts" knows those facts *semantically*—knows them in terms of their meanings (*semantikos*), their inferences and the interpretations of these. In other words, syntax is not metaphysically sufficient for semantics, and "that semantic facts can vary even while the syntactic ones do not" (Melnyk, 1996, p. 395).

It is this dichotomy that the author and the journalist, consciously or not, struggles with in communication with their publics. The most effective journalism is probably long form. More words to play with mean that the author has more capacity to develop the vocabulary that can, more or less successfully, convey the context of the reported facts by suggesting interpretation, explaining significance, bearing empathy and attempting to adhere to the correspondence of knowledge with their object by the insertion of the very forms of semantic "noise" that Shannon's communication theory tries to banish from electronic and digital communication. And in modern print-based journalism, it is from that "noise", making it as rich and as prevalent as possible in the writing, that the basis for a public sphere exists. Here, the facts themselves may be in dispute, but the "fact" of facts as existing somewhere is not. The arguments and the discourses of the public sphere are about interpretation of such facts that are accepted, or about the articulation of more empirically (or semantically) plausible ones to replace them with.

Carol Wilder's essay 'Being Analog' builds upon the work of Watzlawick directly, and upon Hawes and Searle implicitly, to ask: "what is it about the analog that's so seductive, so persuasive, so 'real'?" (1997, p. 252). The problem for Wilder is that:

> The digital level of description, so technologically fundamental to the virtual worlds we now create behind the screen, represents a more abstracted disembodied consciousness, which is at once more expansive and less visceral.
>
> (p. 252)

The digital network, and digital journalism as a product of it, is able to cross time-space in an instant, but, in so doing, it abstracts the communication from nature and from humans in a radical way. What print culture achieved, and increasingly struggled to achieve in more complex analog late-modern modes like radio and television, is what Wilder refers to as a "continuous mapping or coding of experience [evoking] something closer to sensation, authenticity and wholeness" (p. 252). Wilder's "abstracted disembodied consciousness" that is the product of "the digital level of description" is what renders us epistemologically primed to be incredulous towards metanarratives. Lyotard's scepticism is not a bad thing. Enlightenment reason gave us instrumental rationality. And this underpins the logic and obsession with automation—processes that just happen to be made efficient in the extreme by means of computers. Today incredulity towards the uses of computers is notable by its lack.

Lyotard also critiques the technological, political and philosophical basis upon which the modern journalist evolved. This remained stuck in its print culture form for the entire period of modernity. And this worked, more or less, for as long as the world was mostly analog. What the Greeks called *ethos*—or the appeal to authority—was contained in the aura of the printed word. Truth was contained in journalism's ethical code, in the reputation of the journalist and in the prestige of the publication. This was an analog chain of recognition and a grasp of processes of getting to truth that developed over three hundred years. *Ethos* created a place, a space for truth through what Richard Rorty called the "contingency of language", a process where "truth is made rather than found", a truth held in place by the vatic aura of writing until a more persuasively written truth replaces it (1989, p. 3). For the journalist, syntactical language was considered a craft necessity for a literate readership trained to the conventions of written grammar to interpret semantically. And it was these conventions in the heads of a media-literate print culture readership that enabled the politics of the public sphere to conduct itself in something like a democratic fashion.

Online nothing is "made", truth or otherwise, because the journalist's words and images consist of nanoscopic points of light, pixels, discrete, discontinuous and always on the verge of change, contingent upon code and upon the feedback loop that they respond to as part of a vast infrastructural network that no longer has a centre and no source in time-space. This point is important because, to quote Régis Debray (2007, p. 5) again the "material forms and processes through which ideas were transmitted—the communication networks that enable thought to have social existence"—are no longer material, but virtual. The "graphosphere" of print is being overwritten by keyboards and screens. Truths once imputed and held within the printed text now have a vast and virtual and viral social existence of flux that floods the networks as torrents of LED light. The effect upon the material craft of the journalist as truth-teller and storyteller is, frankly, drastic. The journalist Peter Pomerantsev states:

> The grand vessels of old media—books, television, newspapers and radio—that had contained and controlled identity and meaning, who we were and how we talked with one another, how we explained the world to our children, talked about our past, defined war and peace, news and opinion, satire and seriousness, right and left, right and wrong, true, false, realm unreal—these vessels have cracked and burst, breaking up the old architecture of what relates to whom, who speaks to whom and how, magnifying, shrinking, distorting all proportions, sending us in disorienting spirals where words lose shared meaning.
>
> (2019, p. 177)

The covenant between analog writer and reader, one based upon *ethos*, is severely enfeebled within the digital context. The diminished contract exposes the difficulty in assuming any straight transference of the written word from analog to digital without a great loss in fidelity.

Disorienting spirals

In our postmodern culture, the journalist's story seems like it has never been more prevalent in our culture. Narratives are everywhere we look. Many are in long form, of the most excellent syntactical and literary quality, and addressing almost any subject. Such sources of news media data are a keystroke away on our desks; or they will appear with a flick of the forefinger with the phone in our hand; or our voice AI assistant can enable us to magically "stay-in-the-know with Alexa news" in the time it takes you to ask the gadget to connect with the news source of your choice. And, in theory, the story you read or hear read for you by a bot or a journalist may have meaning and truth that's both informative and illuminating. But what your phone or Alexa brings to you needs to be connectable to a larger meaning and truth—to a metanarrative that gives context to your own micro-narrative.

There was a time when the journalist's words would dry in the ambient temperature of a massive print room to became fixed as inkmarks on newsprint paper, there to be produced and reproduced in thousands or millions of near-exact copies. Their daily stories often mirrored the newspaper's editorial line and so were more or less predictable in their politics, their perspective on the truth and the morals and values that the writing carried. The stories were imbued, again more or less, with a vatic authority that stemmed from a long association with a venerable, respected or notorious newspaper, or with newspapers like it or hostile to it. And people you knew read the same stories in the same papers, stories you could discuss with them, at home or work, stories coloured with meanings and truths that came from the semantic shades and nuances that each took from reading the same texts. Over breakfast, on the commute, the lunchtime break, on the return home in the evening, perhaps with the evening edition, millions of people in cities and in nations engaged with print culture. And the engagement, being modern, was also rather deterministic, where, in the words of McLuhan, the reader(s) were connected to "a larger entity of information and perception which forms our thoughts, structures our experience, and determines our views of the world about us" (1975, pp. 74–75). Their feelings and judgements on the news of the day therefore moved in something like unison; rhythmed by the machine industry of modernity, and with their communities, local and national, being recognisable and graspable as entities making up their print-formed public spheres.

Today, once the "publish" button is clicked on the newsroom computer, the words on screen instantly become ones and zeros, bits and bytes of data that dissolve into private corporate databases, there to be converted automatically into "content" whose source (the journalist) is now forever an "abstracted disembodied consciousness" (Wilder, 1997, p. 252) whose vatic authority, such as it is anymore, is highly contingent in a process where keyed in "truths" enter a virtual sphere that's largely unknown and barely mapped, even by the publishers who own the content. Mutability has conquered the erstwhile fixity of words. Words, phrases, sentences, whole stories that once came from the brain and hand of the journalist become a part of something else, *become* something else in their now never-ending journeys through the Internet.

The consumer must *critically reflect and consciously seek* a wider variety in news media, otherwise platforms like Meta and Google, TikTok or X or Telegram, automatically populate their feed for them. News comes in digital streams of discontinuous portions—single articles that come through feeds, notifications, sharing and arbitrary clicks on hyperlinks. The logic, being competitive, is always dynamic and evolving, with speed and efficiency being the watchwords. The innovation of video-based "message news" evolved during the most digital-dominated war in history that followed the Russian invasion of Ukraine in February 2022. And news content, original or endlessly edited and recycled, and with ideological purpose or not and fake or not, can come from anywhere and from anyone at any time. As Meek tells it:

> Smartphones and social media have introduced a third strand of video coverage of dramatic events, the message strand. Though its creators might be focused on particular ends, for viewers, message news is often curated and contextualised by little more than their own prior assumptions and their idiosyncratic, algorithmically influenced collection of messengers. Official and sceptical news still exist, but message news, more intimate and more substantial than mere propaganda, has become a dominant source both for traditional news-gatherers and, directly for us.
>
> (2023, n.p.)

This increasingly sophisticated and dynamic digitalisation of text (including audio and video) creates an irreversible mutability of the sources of truth and fact and what constitutes knowledge. The institutions of media—newspapers, radio and television—with their venerable histories and journalistic achievements have become remediated into competing digital-dominated entities that seek either to gain clicks for advertisers (via the platforms) or to "flood the zone" with disinformation and propaganda (the bad actors). The intent and reputation of the individual journalists notwithstanding, such remediated news content is inescapably adulterated by its technical context. The "grand vessels of old media" have split open (Pomerantsev, 2019, p. 177) and meaning spills forth in great dispersals of data.

This general atomisation of meaning was theorised by Baudrillard in 1983. His cosmic prefiguration's read even better today, given the "black hole" that the Internet would become:

> The social void is scattered with interstitial objects and crystalline clusters which spin around and coalesce in a cerebral chiaroscuro. So is the mass, an *in-vacuo* aggregation of individual particles, refuse of the social and of media impulses: an opaque nebula whose growing density absorbs all the surrounding energy and light rays, to collapse finally under its own weight. A black hole which engulfs the social.
>
> (Baudrillard, 1983, pp. 3–4)

The crisis of meaning is a crisis for politics, too. Partisanship or apathy are the twin dangers. There is no intermediate space where enough reflective and engaged news consumers can use critique and history and moderated reason to chart a path forward, to make a difference and to warn of the dangers of extremism and indifference. Breakthroughs in AI burst onto the public media consciousness in late 2022. But this was simply a coming to public awareness, heightened by hyperbole, of processes that had been going on for decades. One thing is true regarding the potentials and applications of generative AI: it can and will be used to supercharge the negative and toxic forms of news media that have already amplified the legitimation crisis that affects increasingly more of what we read, see and hear. For the first time in history, the provenance and truth of just about everything is now at least potentially suspect. In response, the reflective consumers of news look hopefully for a renaissance in reason; the partisans look towards a strong leader; and the apathetic divert themselves with more entertainment. What were once called the "masses" of the print mass-media age have undergone a profound transformation under the influence of digital. Tiziana Terranova describes the emergence of this now "passive mass" in bleak terms. They (we) are:

> No longer the mass congealed and energized by the containment strategies of the industrial revolution and its disciplinary enclosures, but [instead] a kind of terminal mass – atomized and dispersed at the end of communication receivers, deprived of its revolutionary power in a kind of entropic dispersion.
>
> (2004, p. 136)

If all this negativity on the logic of digital journalism and its online product resonates at least a little with the reality of postmodernity, then we are in trouble.

In a 2013 interview not long before he died, the Uruguayan journalist Eduardo Galeano said, in typically Delphic style: "History never really says goodbye. History says, see you later". What did he mean? He was referring to the political situation across the world, and so he may have been suggesting that fascism could come back to plague us. Alternatively, he may have been feeling rather more optimistic and that the various and largely successful postwar experiments with social democracy could come back in fashion. He didn't elaborate. The thrust of the present book, however, would indicate that the former scenario is the more likely one. Galeano also said: "My great fear is that we are all suffering from amnesia" (Younge, 2013). This time he was clear about the danger that we have forgotten what we can be as moral and ethical agents, and he worried that we no longer realise that we can act as citizens. Forgetting is cognitive, but it is temporal, too. And for most of recorded history both have been shaped by our innate analogicity. Digitality plays tricks on our still-analog sense of time (we tend to dwell in the present); digitality distracts us, and we can easily become shallow thinkers (we outsource much of our knowledge to our devices); and digitality deceives, deludes and determines us (often) (see Hassan, 2009 and 2020).

Humans are anthropologically and technologically incompatible with digital systems they don't fully understand and allow to function with the bare minimum of legislative oversight. The mass beta-testing of humanity with networkable digital products has left us exposed and vulnerable to its inhuman and alienating logic. We are the weak link in the processes of production, with automation seeking constantly to eradicate our fallible and error-prone presence wherever possible. Journalism has been caught up in this drive to anti-human perfection through digital systems, yet it still acts as if it can still function as before. Journalism can't go forward in its modern form, yet it cannot go back; nothing and no one can. And so, journalism, in its modern form, with its traditions of writing, stories, narratives and truth, is being lost to History. That particular History *really has* said goodbye. We just haven't acknowledged that fact yet because, and to stoke Galeano's fear, amnesia comes with the digital territory.

What, then, if anything, can be done?

6 Some conclusions on analog, digital, journalism and truth

Analogs

Digital technology represents the antithesis of what we are as humans. We evolved as a form of technology within a natural ecology of technologies. And it was all analog. We thrived and ultimately dominated due to our facility for originating and developing effective technologies that interacted with our bodies and brains such that: "We become what we behold . . . we shape our tools and afterwards our tools shape us" (Culkin, 1967, p. 54). The body-tool dialectic contained the basis for human survival on earth, for agriculture, settlements, arts, cultures, civilizations. Writing shaped us more than any other technology. Functioning as media, writing meant that "concepts such as meaning, truth, objectivity, accuracy and clarity" became actualised and normative in human communication and action (Williams, 2008, p. 22). Writing gave us History (or the means to record it), and, in the West, that History's path we can pick out and follow towards a particular destination. This was not preordained, but writing, Greek philosophical reason, religion, Renaissance, science, Enlightenment and industrialisation carried us towards what we would call modernity. This was a period of "innovative self-destruction" (Berman, 1982, pp. 98–105), a time of contradictions, especially in its brutal early stages when "everything seems pregnant with its contrary" (Marx, in Bellamy-Foster, 1998, p. 182).

The perceived injustice of the many social and political paradoxes, when faced with the promise of the Enlightenment, is where serious journalism emerged from. Journalism was the knowing yet optimistic spirit of modernity and installed itself as the conscience of the age. It appointed itself as democratic tribune and wrote narratives for "the people" to read and review. Distributed stories became "news" because they conveyed new knowledge, and, as such, they were generally accepted as true—not because they were heard in conversation on the street, or down at the local tavern, but because they were written and printed.

Digital technology obsoleted this venerable analog tradition, along with its forms and processes, built up and legitimated over the generations and centuries and understood by scholars of media history as part of print culture

DOI: 10.4324/9781003054207-7

or print capitalism. Digital has rendered this communicative logic a relic from another time. And classical journalism, lodged intractably at the becoming-redundant core of analog political modernity, is exposed and stranded like a whale in a shallow lagoon. The digital age has no intrinsic need for it and instead commoditizes a postmodernity where stable meaning has imploded. The "masses" increasingly shun the modern metanarratives and presume to think for themselves; they demand spectacle, gadgetry and entertainment; and they are inclined to perceive news as either politically suspect, ideologically biased, corrupted by fakery or simply does not speak to their lives.

Exiles

We have become exiles. Digitality drives us from analog life and compels us into service for the networked economy. There we live and work as digital doubles, avatars of our analog self where exile is felt as a void within (Hassan, 2023, p. 18). Inauthenticity looms as we confront the bleakness of life in front of a screen. It's a synthetic and virtual existence, and we don't know why, really, it is so tiring, so unsatisfying, and why we often feel alone and disconnected within its world of connections. We are "alone together", as the psychologist Sherry Turkle phrased it, with digital connections substituting our social webs of analog physical connections and becoming the "architect of our intimacies" (2017, p. 16). And there are many intimacies that have been reengineered by the experience of looking at a screen. Witness the ubiquity of mobile phones in the hands of individuals in social settings where opportunity for analog sociality is riven by the distractive power of their devices. Reengineered also is the writing of the journalist. In modern times, the "silent privacy, in the lair of the skull" (Anderson, 1983, p. 35) is where thoughts were fixed in print to be transmogrified into subjective feelings in the mind of the reader, and there to be acted out as opinion in a public sphere. Today, infinitely alterable words shimmer on screens as LED representations. There, narratives are compacted into messages, and news endures only for as long as the scroll of blinking text and image is visible on screen. Vatic authority is plagued by the uncertain provenance of words and pictures that exist in an aways-transient present, unfixed in time-space and therefore uncommittable to anything that may endure as knowledge. The modern public sphere as a historically and technologically specific realm of political action cannot exist within such contingency, and so it too has been exiled along with those who once made it possible.

We have been exiled by our governments. In their millions, and through successive generations, citizens have been abandoned to the unpredictable effects of digitality. The neoliberal project was dedicated to opening up modern life to the so-called competition of the free market. "Efficiency" in all things, especially productivity, was the axiom, and computerisation (in all things) would supposedly deliver it. Beginning in the late 1970s, the postwar consensus around the need for a "managed economy" was increasingly dismantled by governments of the right, left and centre as the ideology took hold. The more governments abrogated their responsibilities to market forces, the more the ideology gained power. David Harvey called this process "accumulation by dispossession" (2003, p. 147). He links this dispossession to the sale of public assets like water, energy, transport and government services. Significantly, the privatisation of national communications and media systems was, in effect, *dispossession of, and exile from, a potential digital public sphere* (see Schiller, 2000; Srnicek, 2016). Another form of exile was the dispossession of knowledge as it pertained to our commons of bio-heritage through the licensing of genetic materials and the sequencing of human, animal and plant genomes for commercial purposes. This is "nature's technology" and its colonisation by capital constitutes the commodification of the very stuff that made us analog-technological creatures (Marx, 1982, p. 493, n. 4). The most far-reaching exile of all is through automation, the super-rationalist impulse Jacques Ellul labelled the "exclusion of man" because of our propensity for "error and unpredictability" (1964, p. 136)—unwanted liabilities in the neoliberal ascendancy.

Once upon a time analog-era exiles would find each other in their places of refuge. Political exiles especially would come together to create meaning and solidarity in their exile. As digital exiles we have no real place of refuge. We cannot easily escape that which simultaneously drives us away and draws us in. Digital is omnipresent yet alienating within its own logic. We are channelled by algorithms to become an atomised online collective. Meaning, solidarity and purpose are determined largely by how the algorithm's creators optimise correspondence between users in line with their business model. Algorithmic logic is therefore a problem for a digital public sphere with democratic ambitions. As isolated exiles we are vulnerable to the determinants of algorithms with the power to influence our political-media activity. Our collective isolation produces the virtual embodiment of postmodern space. If we are not made apathetic towards politics, then millions can instead find a virtual home inside the politics of identity. Here, exile finds virtual consolation in the identity group. Online identity politics is factionalised, and identities are encouraged to see themselves as exclusive, as self-contained and as seeing no need to compromise with those perceived to be outsiders—journalist media included. The writing of the modern journalist, the sort that still seeks to speak truth to power, has relatively weak purchase within identity groups where truths tend to be relative and where power, in the form of *identity legitimacy*, is what they seek to acquire, not speak to. The virtual sphere is thus not a public sphere where journalism can meaningfully participate, but a domain of "swarms" of atomised critics, commentators, trollers, influencers, etc., performing as allies or enemies to those whose agendas tend to be angry, narrow-minded and partisan (Han, 2017). The logic of deeply embedded algorithms makes it impossible for such online formations to make themselves inclusive or agonistic in any political meaningful sense.

Truths

To what extent is the written word of the journalist, in print or on screen, still a signifier of truth, of "knowledge corresponding to its object"? To say that it's less than it was even a decade ago seems undeniable. But how much less? It's hard to say. We know the profession suffers from a trust problem. In the United States, it's problem with a long history, beginning in the 1970s after the superlative achievements of Vietnam and Watergate. In a parallel world dominated by print, the decline-of-trust problem is something that could be solved, and the negative trend reversed. Imagine another series of national scandals, an energised public fuelled by journalists exposing political or economic malfeasance and resulting in trials and jail time for the guilty. That could do it. Faith might be restored. But we no longer live in such a world. Digital dominates, and so real-world and *consequential* investigations and public debates are becoming rare. It's notable that the Panama, Paradise and Pandora Papers revelations of 2016, 2017 and 2021, respectively, were prompted by leaks of massive tranches of digital files, with complex interconnections between individuals and institutions involved in corruption, fraud, tax evasion and money laundering. Truths were buried under terabytes of data, numbers, files and spreadsheets. Existing as zeros and ones within hard drives, its truths were of a technologically different kind. Assembled by hundreds of journalists and lawyers into words-as-points-of-light on an LED-backlit screen and released into a dynamically fluctuating news-sphere, any traction with a reading public was short-lived. And soon after each *exposé*, the media cycle moves to something else. The outrages were soon retired to their Wikipedia pages or to the paywalled folios of the *New Yorker* or *Vanity Fair* for the long-from treatment and from there to niche-interest books to be written by future writers and future historians to appear when hardly anyone remembers anymore. Worst of all, the published revelations themselves, storied serially and earnestly in the *Guardian*, the *New York Times*, the *Süddeutsche Zeitung*, and other "partners", had little discernible effect upon the practice of global kleptocracy.

This indecent burial of investigative journalism, under many terabytes of data, gets us back to the question of the main function of the journalist, which is writing and the form it takes today. The mutability of texts, stories and narratives, made vastly more so by advances in AI, means that the provenance of anything can ever be guaranteed; everything is either deniable or affirmable. Fact-checking initiatives like BBC Verify, the *Washington Post*'s Fact Checker, Snopes, Bellingcat and others serve a desperate need, but the fact that they exist at all says something about the perilous state of truth in journalism. And anyway, these are not much more than makeshift efforts. Well-intentioned and valuable they may be, but fact-checker websites are ad hoc initiatives subject to the goodwill of donors and sponsors. The Internet is strewn with dead websites whose donations and/or free labour ran out. Moreover, these demand commitment on the part of the reader too—something that diminishes in the "attention economy". Time spent on newspaper websites in the United States dipped from 2.59 minutes in 2014 to 1.82 in 2020 (Pew, 2021). This suggests we invest less critical reflection in the news we see. And it suggests also that we increasingly scan, skim and surf in the ways that browsers are engineered for us to do (Hassan, 2012). And so in desultory fashion we share, like, dislike or move on without querying the origin or authenticity of much of what we see. Disinformation may well turn up in a still-working fact-checker site, but this does not stop their circulation. It continues on through the networks to become the certified truth of an issue or event or claim for unknown numbers of us. Consciously or unconsciously, we are all implicated in this corruption of modern journalism and the truths it once claimed to present. The postmodern perversion of truth has become the default for millions of us—or enough of us to make a negative difference. Alan Sunderland, a journalist and TV executive, said of this context:

> What does good, traditional journalism do? It seeks out the facts. All of the facts. It carefully weighs those facts to determine as far as possible where the truth lies. It listens to all views, works as hard as it can to identify and eliminate any prejudices or assumptions of its own. It then reports those facts, providing the context required to understand what is being reported. It understands the difference between facts (which are true and verifiable) and opinions, which are the many and varied views about those facts.
>
> Importantly, any balance demonstrated in a good story is a balance that follows the weight of evidence. That's why accuracy and impartiality are forever intertwined: a view that is based on lies or misinformation is either exposed as such or omitted from consideration completely.
>
> Regurgitating the views of others without assessing their factual basis is not journalism.
>
> Balancing a smart well-informed view with an ignorant ill-informed view and giving them the same weight is not journalism.
>
> Failing to care about where the truth lies is not journalism.
>
> (2019)

"Good, traditional journalism" strives to do all these affirmative things. Or it should. Or it did. But today when the "publish" button is clicked on the big, important computer in the depopulated newsroom office, then all that good, ethical, honest (and modern) work is given over instantly to the untender mercies of the postmodern mutability machine.

Political will

In 2023 Eric Horvitz, the chief scientific officer for Microsoft, was moved to state:

> We could be entering a post-epistemic world, where nobody knows what's going on because of the powers of these systems to manipulate … to create alternative realities.
>
> (cited in Marchese, 2023)

To read the quote, then to see the name and occupation of the writer, is an arresting experience. Horvitz's words were written as if from a bystander, as if it had *nothing to do with him*. The quote was cited by the philosopher Daniel Dennett, the subject of a feature titled "How to Live a Happy Life":

> That phrase, the mere fact that [Horvitz] could utter it, is extremely frightening. The presence of agreed-upon landmarks and sources of common knowledge — this is something we've taken for granted for a long time and can no longer take for granted. We have to work to try to restore it.
>
> (cited in Marchese, 2023)

A world may be coming "where nobody knows what's going on", says Horvitz. But he is somebody in a professional role with a platform actively engaged in bringing such a world about. Horvitz expanded upon his work in a 2023 paper titled "Frontier AI Regulation: Managing Emerging Risks to Public Safety" in *arXiv*, a website for open-access research on AI and related technologies:

> Frontier AI models pose a distinct regulatory challenge: dangerous capabilities can arise unexpectedly; it is difficult to robustly prevent a deployed model from being misused; and it is difficult to stop a model's capabilities from proliferating broadly.
>
> (Anderljung et al., 2023: 2)

Dangerous capabilities. Difficult to prevent. Misused. Proliferating broadly. All this in one sentence. Horvitz has a day job, as noted, with Microsoft. A very senior job. With very great responsibilities. His bio tells us that, amongst other duties, his "research endeavours have been direction-setting, including harnessing probability and utility in machine learning and reasoning […] pioneering principles and mechanisms for supporting human-AI collaboration and complementarity" (Microsoft, 2023). It's as if Horvitz's analog self, his science training and method, his experience at the lab workbench, clash in cognitive dissonance with the reality of the digital tools he harnesses for "collaboration and complementarity" towards ends specified, presumably, by Microsoft. Today, with the rush to market of competing versions of AI, from the platforms to the startups, all with a view to marketise whatever capabilities they are purported to have, Horvitz's "collaboration and complementarity" with humans (unless they are tech company shareholders) doesn't seem to be high on anyone's agenda.

In our postmodernity, politics expresses itself, consciously or unconsciously, as the antithesis, or deconstructed reality, of what were the perceived myths of modernity. Stanley Aronowitz noted this particular spectre looming in the late 1980s. Then he saw the neoliberal wave carrying with it "*the rejection of universal reason as the foundation of human affairs*" (1989, p. 49) (italics in the original). This rejection was never professed explicitly in institutional political affairs or on corporate annual reports; rather, it was embedded deep in the neoliberal rhetoric and practice of a *universal market* to where political power had begun to migrate. Aronowitz observed also a discursive shift towards "knowledge and interest, the latter being understood as a 'standpoint' from which to grasp 'reality'" (p. 49). This was a postmodern abandonment of "scientificity" or "science as a set of propositions claiming validity by any given competent investigatory [sic]" (p. 49). In other words, the logic and reason that had universalised modernity and the political institutions that helped shape it were giving way to the "knowledge and interest" of precisely those engaged in the neoliberal globalisation project. This new discursive logic attacked the "impartial competence" (p. 49) of governments to work for the benefit of everyone in a national-democratic context and is dismissed as merely the sectional interests of the old ways of thinking that excluded women, non-white ethnicities and cultures and much of the rest of the world outside of the metropolitan centres of Euro-America. Maybe it did. Globalisation would change that. But not in a way reckoned with by many. The modern "impartial competence" that was already dissolving by the 1980s,has almost gone today. "Impartial" now means letting the market decide; and "competence" is understood as making the domestic economy amenable to global capital through lower taxes, weak or non-existent labour organisation and the "right" of managers to manage as they see fit.

Today political will of the kind that could shape the nation according to the needs of popular will no longer exists in any meaningful sense. Political action has become increasingly performative, something to promise or discuss or have an inquiry about at some time. Ordinarily such inertia would be a boon to a critical journalism that speaks truth to power. But journalism's own power has been deeply curtailed—and compromised. Digitalisation, automation and all the things we've already considered has left the profession hanging by a thread, dependent upon the goodwill of a shrinking demographic of baby boomer subscribers and searching for ways to make paywalls pay.

In Australia, in 2020, an apparent outbreak of political will on the part of the federal government to "get tough" with Meta and Google offered a potential solution to at least some of the woes of both journalists and newsrooms. Since their inception, platforms like Facebook have been using news content from newspapers for free. Facebook users share content, fake or otherwise, with their connections, who can do likewise, and so free content proliferates. Such was the attraction of free content on social media, it rapidly became where most people in many countries got their news from (Forman-Katz & Matza, 2022). News media got nothing from this massive copying of their content. Moreover, the platforms had been attracting much of the advertising that had once gone to the newspapers, and the newspaper's own websites were proving less attractive than news content created for them by platform algorithms. This is still a major headache for legacy media owners across the world. Something had to give.

This is where political will needs to be qualified. In this story, it was less "impartial competence" on the part of the Australian federal government than it was partisan pressure from Rupert Murdoch's News Corp, that "helped persuade the Australian parliament to pass a law that [compelled] Facebook and Google to pay substantial sums … to news organisations whose headlines frequently appear on platforms' pages" (Grueskin, 2022). This was real money that helped newspapers hire journalists and editors, especially in the rural areas where the local press had been decimated. Details of the deals are "murky", Grueskin observes, and they are closely guarded by both parties. Moreover, only the major newspapers are involved, with content from smaller newspapers still receiving nothing from the platforms. This inequality is just part of it. The big newspapers in on the deal, like the *Guardian*, have become *dependent* on Google and Facebook for much of their traffic. And dependency has a price. First, it means that platform-directed users tend to read a lot of "message news", disconnected content, not the longer, connected content of the online newspaper itself. This is bad for narratives and for stories as the means of understanding an issue in an informed way. Second, there is the temptation for newspapers to anticipate the kind of snippet content users read via the platforms, like sport, crime, violence, entertainment and so on, and to produce more of it. This would reduce newspapers to the kind of spectacle-providers that Baudrillard warned of, where the "masses" know what they want, and it's not political engagement through a public sphere but distraction from unspectacular lives (Terranova, 2004, pp. 135–136). Third, this is a cheap deal for the platforms (around $200 million in a year). And Grueskin tells us the platforms can walk away from the deal whenever it suits them, knowing there's nothing much the newspapers or government can do about it. Google, Meta and others do receive financial penalties in the European Union and elsewhere for infringement of various laws pertaining to their content but appeals often take years. The immensely rich platforms can afford it—newspapers can't. Grueskin quotes Matt Nicholl, editor of the *Cape York Weekly* in far north Queensland on the subject of dependency, who puts it candidly: "What if Google decides it's a bad deal for them? If you need Google funding to prop up your journalism, to keep your journalists employed, that's not sustainable" (Grueskin, 2022).

This is how political will functions today in respect of the fourth estate: governments don't have much of it, whereas several decades of neoliberalism have turned the platforms into significant political actors who can

> sell their power to persuade to the highest bidder, whether advertisers, governments and/or political parties, which have come to rely on the infrastructure of platforms to communicate with their customers, citizens and/or voters.
>
> (Helberger, 2020, p. 846)

So not only are newspapers in thrall to the platforms, but so also are governments in liberal democracies—that is if they want to have at least some control over their messaging to an atomised citizenry they can now no longer easily reach otherwise.

Governance

In *Internet for the People*, technology writer Ben Tarnoff writes: “To build a better internet, we need to change how it is owned and organised” (2022, p. vx). He continues:

> The present order of things is not merely unfair. It is fundamentally undemocratic. What is at stake is nothing less than the possibility of democracy—a possibility that an internet organized by the profit motive precludes.
>
> (p. 33)

There is no shortage of arguments declaring that an ever-sprawling Internet needs effective democratic governance (e.g., Bygrave & Bing, 2009; DeNardis, 2014; UNESCO, 2017; Helberger, 2020). The internet was conceived as a 1980s free market experiment, delivered by investor capital, on the back of research funded by U.S. taxpayers going back to the late 1960s. Effective governance over new communications technology has failed to materialise, notwithstanding the ever-greater need for it. This lack is the most serious challenge journalism faces. The magnitude of the problem, and the need for some kind of external authority to instil reason and restraint over runaway developments in AI systems with “human-competitive intelligence”, is now urgent. This was recognised in the widespread shock and awe over the release of OpenAI’s GPT-3 application in late 2022. An Open Letter, dated March 2023, and signed by many in the Euro-American research community, warned that “AI could represent a profound change in the history of life on Earth, and should be planned for and managed with commensurate care and resources” (FOLI, 2023). It called for a worldwide six-month “pause” on research so developers and policymakers could “dramatically accelerate [the] development of robust AI governance systems”. If a pause were not implemented voluntarily by industry, then “governments should step in and institute a moratorium” (FOLI, 2023). A pause was not implemented, and no government stepped in.

Policymakers and AI developers work globally, and independently, in countries all around the world. Multilateral discussions do take place but often in a strange otherworldly context. For instance, in 2019 the Organisation for Economic Co-operation and Development (OECD) set out a policy wish list titled: "Artificial Intelligence: OECD Principles". "Organisations and individuals" were urged to sign up to a set of nebulous principles, like "Human Centred Values and Fairness" (OECD, 2019). There was nothing to stop OpenAI from uploading its GPT app to hundreds of millions of devices a few short years later; and none of its competitors sought to impose a moratorium on themselves after the publication of the Open Letter.

Such feebleness speaks of a disconnect between policymakers and the computer sector. And like the atrophy of institutional political will, its roots lie in our neoliberal history. Wendy Brown tells us in *Undoing the Demos* that colonisation by the logic of competition, as opposed to exchange, has inserted a "market instrumental rationality" between democracy and the proper functioning of the state (2015, p. 41). She asks:

> What happens to rule by and for the people when neoliberal reason configures both soul and city as contemporary firms, rather than as polities? What happens to the constituent elements of democracy — its culture, subjects, principles, and institutions — when neoliberal rationality saturates political life?
>
> (p. 27)

When instrumental rationality permeates the political process together with the "soul and city" it is meant to speak for, then what Brown calls "political rationality" (p. 36) becomes default for the "economizing [of] the state" (p. 32), where the state and its responsibilities are regarded as on a par with corporations. This is doubtless correct, but Brown writes as a political theorist, and so her arguments are limited in their potential insight. She does not mention digital technology; she does not even refer to communications, let alone journalism. Yet these are vital realms for fully understanding the disconnect she describes so eloquently. Computers are both cause and consequence of "market instrumental rationality". Moreover, their "discontinuous" logic breaks up the "continuous" analog communication linkages that once held modern society together. How do people find each other by means of the new "political rationality"? They "diagonalise" through a social media that *cuts across* the old analog lines of communication:

> Born in part through transformations in technology and communication, diagonalists tend to contest conventional monikers of left and right (while generally arcing toward far-right beliefs), to express ambivalence if not

> cynicism toward parliamentary politics, and to blend convictions about holism and even spirituality with a dogged discourse of individual liberties.
>
> (Callison & Slobodian, 2021)

Mainstream media and journalists are seen as part of the problem by the "diagonalists" and so are largely shunned. Instead, they form themselves into "hostile counterpublics, agents of 'disinfotainment', social movements of rabbit holes [and] gig conspiracies for the gig economy" (Callison & Slobodian, 2021). People and politics become disengaged from the wellspring of what used to be called "political imagination". This lack of capacity to envisage alternative worlds, a post-capitalist world, is tangible today. Wolfgang Streeck, for example, argues that information technology has "destroyed the working class [and is now] about to destroy the middle class as well" (2016, p. 9). The focus by most philosophers and political scientist's on Streeck's question: "how will capitalism end?" is depressingly narrow, with communications of any kind—not least journalism—barely mentioned. As Wendy Brown writes, chronically lacking in a modern and Enlightenment-derived imagination, with its narratives and metanarratives of political progress and democratic citizenship, we

> cannot see the ways in which we have lost a recognition of ourselves as held together by literatures, images, religions, histories, myths, ideas, forms of reason, grammars, figures, and languages. Instead, we are presumed to be held together by technologies and capital flows. That presumption, of course, is at risk of becoming true, at which point humanity will have entered its darkest chapter ever. We would be the entities of human capital, and nothing else, of the contemporary economic theoretical imagination.
>
> (2015, p. 188)

Postscript on the automation trap

Our predicament boils down to automation. For all of our prehistory and almost all of our recorded history, humans acted as technological creatures within an ecology of technology. In an environment comprised of the natural world, animals and materials of wood, stone, metals and so on, we lived adaptively and dynamically in and through this ecology to become the apex species. We became special through our evolved facility for technology. We became technology—analog technology—that was analogous with the natural world and its materials. We just didn't know it.

To get to the stage of automation, we first created a technology based on the way we communicate—writing technologised spoken words. And so with the invention of cuneiform writing almost four thousand years ago, we invented a future trap. Again, we didn't know it and it wasn't preordained. But the ancient Greeks, the first significant beneficiaries of writing in the West, were able to build the first computer, the Antikythera Machine, analog of course, that analogised the known stars and planets through an exquisite array of cogs and wheels and pointers that represented the known extraterrestrial movements. Aristotle dreamed of a world where robots would do the work of craftsmen and slaves. And so with working analog computers and a rudimentary automaton, the Greeks brought the trap from the abstract to the real; humans had conceived of being able to release themselves from the burden of physical and mental labour, and they wrote about it and built a machine that would one day realise the dream.

But with the thousand year interregnum from the fall of Rome to the Renaissance, the dream and the written records of automation were lost. The gap was an Arcadian time-space where writing was religious, machines were rare and the analog human was at his embodied raw peak as *Homo faber*. Mind and body worked as part of an analog world that was recognisable to them and was literally to hand. It was a time when, as Anthony Grafton (2022) puts it:

> Artisans came to understand their work as a key to natural processes more generally: not a modern discipline, systematic and skeptical in its approach and aiming at conceptual clarity and clear results, but something older, richer, and more complicated. Craftsmen connected the elements with the heavens, their work with their health, the metals that grew in the earth with the temperaments that governed their bodies.

It's an evocative micro-picture of premodern life. A wholly different conceptual universe materialises where Gehlen's process of co-constitution in the relationship with technology "goes through object, eye, and hand and which in returning to the object concluded itself and begins anew" (1980, p. 19). Life may well have been "nasty, brutish and short" for many, or most, but it would have contained very different and possibly more rewarding ways of being and seeing; ways that are only recently being unearthed and imagined by historians and anthropologists like Grafton.

The fall of Constantinople in 1453 prompted an exodus of classical Greek scholars, along with their ancient texts, to cities like Venice and Florence, where they helped launch the Renaissance. Gutenberg was already printing indulgences in Mainz, and by 1494 the Venetian Aldus Manutius was printing the works of Aristotle and pocket editions of Greek classics that were so popular they were immediately pirated. When the rediscovered Greek ideas took off, so did we rekindle our relationship with technology. Print and literacy spread Francis Bacon's scientific method, and European society soon reached the foothills of modernity. Its science was mostly applied and concerned with mathematics, mechanism and industrial ends that would feed into the needs of a nascent capitalism (Gaukroger, 2006). Bacon himself had specific ideas about what his method meant not only for technology, but for what it would mean to be human, too. In his *Novum Organon* (1620) Bacon argued that guided by science:

> the entire work of the mind [will] be started over again; and from the very start the mind should not be left to itself but be constantly controlled; and the business done … by machines … [And] in any major work that the human hand undertakes, the strength of individuals cannot be increased nor the forces of all united without the aid of tools and machines.
>
> (2000, pp. 28–29)

He foresaw machines coming to our aid, extending our power over nature, and automation controlling our mind and body. The automation trap that was embryonic in the scientific method is something we see today in a process Bacon hinted at: the *automation of science*, or, leaving it to computers or AI to "find" new ideas as "undiscovered links between [informational] nodes" (Alkhateeb, 2017). The trap, being in the idea itself, was opened for us to enter at the dawn of the modern age. With society inside, it began to close gradually with every innovation towards automation brought forth as *technology* (Hui, 2016, p. 4, n. 3). For most of our history, humans brought forth the technological solutions thought necessary for that many and varied human problems. But with modernity, the criteria for what was necessary were stipulated by those ends in the service of capitalism. And so with each new advance in automation, the trap would close by itself. To date, the Internet is the most spectacular example of a human-made digital enclosure, carved out of virtual space and into which we in our billions migrated to act through our digital representations as avatars of our alienated analog selves.

It didn't have to be like this. But specific choices were made in the late modern period, mainly by Cold War–era politicians, physicists, mathematicians and computer engineers, all of whom served to lock in a path of development towards digitality. The "closed world" (Edwards, 1996) of research into automation in the form of military command-and-control systems was created with little or no input from civil institutions that could have questioned the unfolding logic. It was a logic that would construct a secret Internet, and then that technology would be given for free to corporations to develop further for their own needs. Its needs were also a form of command and control—to exploit people as sources of profit, as data points for the harvesting of their activity, thoughts, writing, movements, purchases, etc. that would underwrite ever more powerful algorithmic systems that repeat the process. Automation wherever possible was a necessary component of the business plan. "Accumulate, accumulate! That is the Moses and the Prophets". Marx wrote this mocking exhortation in *Capital* to describe the central motive force of mid-19th-century capitalism (Marx, 1967, p. 595). Today, "automate, automate!" serves the same function of capitalism's leading edges of computerisation, and its profit imperative permeates almost everything as the "closed world" of military rationality opens ever wider to encompass economy, culture and society.

Again, it didn't need to be like this. Promising alternatives were mooted in the "closed world" days that would keep the human in control of computer systems in order to "humanise" them. Another Macy Conference veteran, J.C.R. Licklider, wrote an influential paper titled "Man-Computer Symbiosis" in 1960. It argued for a "symbiotic partnership" between computers and humans where "men (sic) will set the goals, formulate the hypothesis and perform the evaluations" (1960, p. 4). Within the "closed world" context, "partnership", not profitability, was the main concern, one based upon effective "intellectual" processes (p. 4). He could have scarcely envisaged an Internet-dominated planet where profitability—by means of the automation of the human role—would be a fundamental driver. Just as penetrating, though hardly any more promising, was the philosophical apprehension that emerged in the writings of Norbert Wiener, also a Macy veteran, in his speculations on the military uses of the cybernetic systems he developed for the U.S. military in the 1940s. Automation drove the command-and-control systems he helped develop. But he saw grave dangers ahead as computing became more advanced and powerful. In his 1954 book *The Human Use of Human Beings*, he argued:

> Let us remember that the automatic machine, whatever we think of any feelings it may have or may not have, is the precise economic equivalent of slave labor. Any labor which competes with slave labor must accept the economic conditions of slave labor.
>
> (p. 164)

Licklider and Wiener were influential scientists and philosophers, but their dreams and nightmares proved irrelevant to the hard realities of Cold War strategic thinking and, later, the profit potential of previously military technology spreading through the open economy.

The logic of human individual control, or social partnership in our relationship with computers, is, despite the rhetoric of Silicon Valley, utterly peripheral to their actual practical concerns. Computers are designed to control and manipulate environments and people. And they do, mostly, and for much of our time. But social-based control of some kind *will* come. Things have gone too far in too many domains. What this control will look like and if it will be effective is too soon to say. Whether this will be liberal market governments trying to appease the platforms with relatively pain-free "guardrails" that they will accept or multilateral organisations like the EU that will seek to bludgeon the platforms into submission with the threat of increasing financial penalties and sanctions that will eventually enforce positive, human and democratic change is not yet clear.

Another approach is possible. It comes out of a deep reconsideration of our relationship with technology. We must piece together the human history of technology from the perspective of the distinction between analog and digital and seek to understand our relationship to each. We must recognise that the arrival of digital systems as default for almost everything means that much of human activity is conducted through a technology that constitutes more than something that is merely "different". It constitutes a *new category* of technology that expresses a very different logic to that which it replaces. We must understand that. So much has changed already, especially change in how we communicate. And the medium, more than ever, is the message. But it's a message still in a bottle.

So, what is digital's "message"?

Well, it's more a piece of advice: "we must know ourselves better", as Nietzsche wrote.

More philosophy and anthropology are necessary to do this—so to recognise what media is today. To see ourselves as cause and consequence of media's forms, processes and categories will help us better understand human-technological practice and what we have gained and lost in the precipitate leap from analog to digital. Then we will know ourselves better.

And, perhaps like Samuel Johnson's archetypal journalist, we can communicate our truths as widely as possible so that we all will know with a little more certainty, "how the world goes; who rises, and who falls; who triumphs, and who is defeated".

Bibliography

Abel, D. (1942). The significance of the letter to the Abbé Raynal in the progress of Thomas Paine's thought. *The Pennsylvania Magazine of History and Biography, 66*(2), 176–190. https://doi.org/10.2307/20087476

Adorno, T., and Horkheimer, M. (2002). *Dialectic of enlightenment.* Stanford: Stanford University Press.

Alkhateeb, A. (2017, April 27). Science has outgrown the human mind and its limited capacities. *The Wire.* https://thewire.in/science/science-outgrown-human-mind-limited-capacities

Anderlijung, M. et al. (2023). Frontier AI regulation: Managing emerging risks to public safety. *arXiv.* https://arxiv.org/abs/2307.03718

Anderson, B. (1983). *Imagined communities: Reflections on the origin and spread of nationalism.* London: Verso.

Andreotti, O. (Ed.). (2015). *Journalism at risk: Threats, challenges and perspectives.* Strasbourg: Council of Europe.

Appadurai, A. (1990). Disjuncture and difference in the global cultural economy. In M. Featherstone (Ed.), *Global culture: Nationalism, globalization and modernity* (pp. 295–310). London: Sage.

Arendt, H. (1967, February 25). Truth and politics. *The New Yorker.* https://www.newyorker.com/magazine/1967/02/25/truth-and-politics

Aronowitz, S. (1989). Postmodernism and politics. *Social Text, 21*, 46–62. https://doi.org/10.2307/827808

Ascherson, N. (2022, October 23). Neal Ascherson at 90: 'Journalism was easier in my time. You had more time to think.' *The Guardian.* Retrieved from https://www.theguardian.com/books/2022/oct/23/neal-ascherson-at-90-journalism-interview

Australian Senate Government. (2017). Senate select committee on the future of public interest journalism. Parliament of Australia. https://www.aph.gov.au/Parliamentary_Business/Committees/Senate/Future_of_Public_Interest_Journalism

Bacon, F. (2000). *The new organon.* Cambridge: Cambridge University Press.

Balz, D. (2022, June 12). Watergate happened 50 years ago. *The Washington Post.* https://www.washingtonpost.com/politics/2022/06/12/watergate-trust-government-reforms

Barthes, R. (1968). *Elements of semiology.* New York: Hill and Wang.

Baudrillard, J. (1983). *In the shadow of the silent majorities or, the end of the social and other essays.* Cambridge, MA: MIT Press.

Bell, D. (1973). *The coming of post-industrial society.* London: Heinemann Educational Books.

Bellamy-Foster, J. (1998). *The communist manifesto now*. Socialist Register 1998. Leo Panitch and Colin Leys (Eds.). Milton Keynes (UK): The Merlin Press.

Bergson, H. (1950). *Time and free will*. London: George Allen and Unwin.

Bergson, H. (2001). *Time and free will: An essay on the immediate data of consciousness*. Mineola, NY: Dover Publications.

Berman, M. (1982). *All that is solid melts into air*. London: Verso.

Bolter, J. D., & Grusin, R. (1999). *Remediation: Understanding new media*. Cambridge, MA: MIT Press.

Boyer, G. R. (2021). *The winding road to the welfare state: Economic insecurity and social welfare policy in Britain*. Princeton, NJ: Princeton University Press.

Brenan, M. (2022, October 18). *Americans' trust in media remains near record low*. Gallup. https://news.gallup.com/poll/403166/americans-trust-media-remains-near-record-low.aspx

Brown, W. (2015). *Undoing the demos: Neoliberalism's stealth revolution*. New York: Zone Books.

Bruner, J. (1991). The narrative construction of reality. *Critical Inquiry, 18*(1), 1–21. https://doi.org/10.2307/1343711

Burke, P. (2012). *A social history of knowledge II: From the Encyclopedia to Wikipedia*. Cambridge, MA: Polity.

Butler, J. (1998). Merely cultural. *New Left Review, I*(227), 33–44. https://doi.org/10.2307/466744

Bygrave, L. A., & Bing, J. (2009). *Infrastructure and institutions*. Oxford: Oxford University Press.

Callison, W., & Slobodian, Q. (2021, January 12). Coronapolitics from the Reichstag to the Capitol. *Boston Review*. https://www.bostonreview.net/articles/quinn-slobodian-toxic-politics-coronakspeticism/

Candelaria, K. (2010). A postmodern view of morality in the works of Morrison, Capote, and O'Brien (OCLC Number: 669982956) [Master's thesis, The California State University]. https://scholarworks.calstate.edu/concern/theses/1544bp77t

Capote, T. (1966). *In cold blood*: New York: Random House.

Chomsky, N. (1978). *Topics in the theory of generative grammar*. Boston, MA: De Gruyter.

Chomsky, N. (1993). *Language and thought*. Wakefield, RI & London: Moyer Bell.

Coates, T. (2015). *Between the world and me*. New York: Spiegel & Grau.

Colvin, M. (2010). *Truth at all costs*. Marie Colvin Memorial Foundation. https://mariecolvin.org/truth-at-all-costs-marie-colvin

Culkin, J. M. (1967). A schoolman's guide to Marshall McLuhan. *The Saturday Review*, 51–53, 70–72. https://webspace.royalroads.ca/llefevre/wp-content/uploads/sites/258/2017/08/A-Schoolmans-Guide-to-Marshall-McLuhan-1.pdf

Darnton, R. (1979). *The business of enlightenment: A publishing history of the Encyclopédie 1775–1800*. Cambridge and London: Belknap Press.

David, M. (2015, May 28). *The correspondence theory of truth*. Stanford Encyclopedia of Philosophy. https://plato.stanford.edu/entries/truth-correspondence/

Davies, N. (2008). *Flat earth news: An award-winning reporter exposes falsehood, distortion and propaganda in the global media*. London: Chatto & Windus.

Debord, G. (2014). *The society of the spectacle*. Berkeley, CA: Bureau of Public Secrets.

Debray, R. (2007). Socialism: A life-cycle. *New Left Review, 46*, 5–17.

Deleuze, G. (1983). *Nietzsche and philosophy*. London: Athlone.

DeNardis, L. (2014). *The global war for internet governance*. New Haven, CT: Yale University Press.

Derrida, J. (1967). *Of grammatology*. Baltimore and London: John Hopkins University Press.

Deuze, M. (2019). What journalism is (not). *Social Media + Society*, *5*(3), 1–4. https://doi.org/10.1177/2056305119857202.

Dewey, J. (2012). *The public and its problems: An essay in political inquiry*. Pennsylvania, PA: Penn State University Press.

Edwards, P. N. (1996). *The closed world: Computers and the politics of discourse in cold war America*. Cambridge, MA: MIT Press.

EAFR. (2023). *The first television war*. Encyclopedia of American Foreign Policy. https://www.americanforeignrelations.com/O-W/Television-The-first-television-war.html

Eisenstein, E. L. (1979). *The printing press as an agent of change and the structure of communications revolutions*. New York: Cambridge University Press.

Eisenstein, E. L. (2002). An unacknowledged revolution revisited. *The American Historical Review*, *107*(1), 87–105. https://doi.org/10.1086/532098

Elegant, R. (1981). How to lose a war: The press and Viet Nam. *Encounter*, *57*(2), 73–90. http://academics.wellesley.edu/Polisci/wj/Vietnam/Readings/elegant.htm

Ellul, J. (1964). *The technological society*. New York: Vintage.

Estévez, S. (2009). Is nostalgia becoming digital?: Ecuadorian diaspora in the age of global capitalism. *Social Identities*, *15*(3), 393–410. https://doi.org/10.1080/13504630902899366

Falk, R. (1988). Appropriating tet. *The Massachusetts Review*, *29*(3), 391–420. https://doi.org/10.2307/25090001

Fisk, R. (1990). *Pity the nation: Lebanon at war*. Oxford: Oxford University Press.

FOLI. (2023, March 22). *Pause giant AI experiments: An open letter*. Future of Life Institute. https://futureoflife.org/open-letter/pause-giant-ai-experiments/

Forman-Katz, N., & Matsa, K. E. (2022, September 20). *News platform fact sheet*. Pew Research Center. https://www.pewresearch.org/journalism/fact-sheet/news-platform-fact-sheet/

Foucault, M. (1977). The political function of the intellectual. *Radical Philosophy*, *017*(Summer), 12–14.

Fraser, N. (1990). Rethinking the public sphere: A contribution to the critique of actually existing democracy. *Social Text*, *25/26*(56), 56–80. https://doi.org/10.2307/466240

Friedman, M. (1962). *Capitalism and freedom*. Chicago, IL: University of Chicago Press.

Fukuyama, F. (1995). *Trust: The social virtues and the creation of prosperity*. New York: The Free Press.

Gall, C., & De Waal, T. (1997). *Chechnya: A small victorious war*. London: Pan Books.

Gates, B. (1996). *The road ahead*. New York: Viking Penguin.

Gaukroger S. (2006). *The emergence of a scientific culture. Science and the shaping of modernity, 1210–1685*, Oxford: Oxford University Press.

Gehlen, A. (1980). *Man in the age of technology*. New York: Columbia University Press.

Gerard, R. W. (1953). Some of the problems concerning digital notions in the central nervous system. Eighth Macy Conference. http://pcp.vub.ac.be/books/gerard.pdf.

Giddens, A. (1990). *The consequences of modernity*. Stanford, CA: Stanford University Press.

Grafton, A. (2022, September 22). How to cast a metal lizard. *The New York Review*. https://www.nybooks.com/articles/2022/09/22/artisanal-work-discovery-knowledge-anthony-grafton/

Gray, J. (2003). *Straw dogs: Thoughts on humans and other animals*. London: Granta Books.

Grubb, G. G. (1941). On the serial publication of Oliver Twist. *Modern Language Notes*, *56*(4), 290–294. https://doi.org/10.2307/2910445

Grueskin, B. (2022, March 9). Australia pressured Google and Facebook to pay for journalism. *Columbia Journalism Review*. https://www.cjr.org/business_of_news/australia-pressured-google-and-facebook-to-pay-for-journalism-is-america-next.php

Habermas, J. (1981). Modernity versus Postmodernity. *New German Critique*, *22*(3). https://doi.org/10.2307/487859

Habermas, J. (1989). *The structural transformation of the public sphere*. Cambridge, MA: Polity.

Hall, S. (2010). The life and times of the first new left. *New Left Review*, *6*, 177–195.

Hammond, W. M. (1989). The press in Vietnam as agent of defeat: A critical examination. *Reviews in American History*, *17*(2), 312–323. https://doi.org/10.2307/2702936

Han, B. (2017). *In the swarm: Digital prospects*. Cambridge, MA: MIT Press.

Harari, Y. N. (2014). *Sapiens: A Brief history of humankind*. New York: Signal.

Haraway, D. (1985). Manifesto for cyborgs: science, technology, and socialist feminism in the 1980s. *Socialist Review*, *80*, 65–108.

Hardy, B. (1968). Towards a poetics of fiction: An approach through narrative. *Novel*, *2*, 5–14.

Harvey, D. (1982). *Limits to capital*. Chicago, IL: University of Chicago Press.

Harvey, D. (1989). *The condition of postmodernity: An enquiry into the origins of cultural change*. Oxford: Blackwell.

Harvey, D. (2003). *The new imperialism*. Oxford: Oxford University Press.

Harvey, D. (2011). *The enigma of capital*. London: Profile Books.

Hassan, R. (2009). *Empires of speed: Time and the acceleration of politics and society*. Leiden: Brill.

Hassan, R. (2012). *The Age of distraction: Reading, writing, and politics in a high-speed networked economy*. New Brunswick: Transaction Publishers.

Hassan, R. (2020). *The condition of digitality: A post-modern Marxism for the practice of digital life*. London: University of Westminster Press.

Hassan, R. (2023). *Analog*. Cambridge, MA: MIT Press.

Hawes, L. (2015). *A new philosophy of social conflict*. London: Bloomsbury.

Hayles, N. K. (1999). *How we became posthuman: Virtual bodies in cybernetics, literature, and informatics*. Chicago, IL: University of Chicago Press.

Heidegger, M. (1977). *The question concerning technology and other essays*. New York and London: Garland Publishing.

Helberger, N. (2020). The political power of platforms: How current attempts to regulate misinformation amplify opinion power. *Digital Journalism*, *8*(6), 842–854.

Herman, E. S., & Chomsky, N. (1988). *Manufacturing consent: The political economy of the mass media*. New York: Pantheon Books.

Hitchens, C. (2000). Introduction. In E. Waugh (Ed.), *Scoop* (p. 176). New York: Penguin.
Hitchens, C. (2008). *Thomas Paine's rights of man: A biography*. New York: Grove Press.
Hobsbawm, E. (1996). *The age of revolution: 1789–1848*. New York: Vintage.
Hobsbawm, E. (1999). *Industry and empire: From 1750 to the present day*. New York: New Press.
Hui, Y. (2016). *The question concerning technology in China*. Cambridge, MA: MIT Press.
Husserl, E. (1964). *The phenomenology of internal time consciousness*. The Hague: Martinus Nijhoff.
IFJ. (2020). *White paper on global journalism*. International Federation of Journalists. https://www.ifj.org/fileadmin/user_upload/IFJ_white_book__part_1.pdf
Jaeggi, R. (2014). *Alienation*. New York: Columbia University Press.
Jaynes, J. (1976). *The origin of consciousness in the breakdown of the bicameral mind*. Boston, MA: Houghton Mifflin.
Johnson, S. (1755). *A dictionary of the English language*. Great Britain: Consortium.
Johnson, S. (1758). *Of the duty of a journalist*. Yale Digital Edition of the Works of Samuel Johnson. http://www.yalejohnson.com/frontend/sda_viewer?n=112293
Johnston, J. (2010). *The allure of machinic life*. Cambridge, MA: MIT Press.
Joseph, P. (2017, September 20). Lessons from the living room war. *Tufts Now*. https://now.tufts.edu/2017/09/20/lessons-living-room-war
Kahneman, D. (2011). *Thinking, fast and slow*. New York: Farrar, Straus and Giroux.
Kant, E. (2007). *Critique of pure reason*. New York: Penguin.
Kant, E. (2009). Idea for a universal history from a cosmopolitan point of view. In A. Rorty & J. Schmidt (Eds.), *Kant's idea for a universal history with a cosmopolitan aim: A critical guide* (pp. 9–23). Cambridge: Cambridge University Press.
Karnow, S. (1997). *Vietnam: A history*. New York: Penguin.
Kaufmann, S. (1966, January 22). Capote in Kansas. The New Republic. https://newrepublic.com/article/114887/stanley-kauffmann-truman-capotes-cold-blood
Kennedy, D. (2002). *Helen Maria Williams and the age of revolution*. Lewisburg: Bucknell University Press.
Kern, S. (1983). *The culture of time and space: 1880–1918*. Cambridge: Harvard University Press.
Kolko, J. (1988). *Restructuring the world economy*. New York: Pantheon Books.
Lakoff, G., & Johnson, M. (1980). *Metaphors we live by*. Chicago, IL: University of Chicago Press.
Lash, S., & Urry, J. (1987). *The end of organized capital*. Cambridge: Polity.
Leibniz, G. W. (2012). *Philosophical papers and letters*. Amsterdam: Kluwer Academic Publishers.
Lefever, E. W. (1974). *TV and national defense: An analysis of CBS News, 1972–1973*. Boston, VA: Institute for American Strategy.
Licklider, J. C. R. (1960). Man–computer symbiosis. *IRE Transactions on Human Factors in Electronics*, *1*, 4–11.
Lilly, P. (2020). 'Windows came out 25 years ago and it was a game-changer for PCs'. https://www.pcgamer.com/happy-birthday-windows-95/
Lippmann, W. (2012). *Public opinion*. New York: Dover Publications.

Littleton, S. M. (1992). *The Wapping dispute: An examination of the conflict and its impact on the national newspaper industry*. Aldershot: Avebury.

Lyotard, J. F. (1979). *The postmodern condition: A report on knowledge*. Manchester: Manchester University Press.

Macintyre, D. (2016). It was, oh yes it was. *British Journalism Review*, *27*(2), 31–37. https://doi.org/10.1177/0956474816652812

Marchese, D. (2023, August 25). How to live a happy life, from a leading atheist. *The New York Times*. https://www.nytimes.com/interactive/2023/08/27/magazine/daniel-dennett-interview.html

Marcuse, H. (2002). *One-dimensional man: Studies in the ideology of advanced industrial society*. London and New York: Routledge.

Marx, K. (1967). *Capital*. New York: International Publishers.

Marx, K. (1973). *Grundrisse*. New York: Penguin.

Marx, K. (1982). *Capital: A critique of political economy* (Vol. 1). New York: Penguin.

Marx, K. (1992). *The poverty of philosophy*. New York: International Publishers.

Marx, K., & Engels, F. (1976). The manifesto of the Communist Party. In *Selected Works*. Moscow: Progress Press.

McAfee, A., & Brynjolfsson, E. (2014). *The second machine age: Work, progress, and prosperity in a time of brilliant technologies*. New York: W. W. Norton & Company.

McChesney, R. W. (2013). *Digital disconnect: How capitalism is turning the internet against democracy*. New York: New Press.

McChesney, R. W., & Nichols, J. (2010). *The death and life of American journalism: The media revolution that will begin the world again*. Philadelphia: Nation Books.

McLuhan, M. (1962). *The Gutenberg galaxy: The making of the typographic man*. Toronto: University of Toronto Press.

McLuhan, M. (1975). McLuhan's laws of the media. *Technology and Culture*, *16*(1), 74–78.

McQuillan, M. (Ed.). (2000). *The narrative reader*. London and New York: Routledge.

Meek, J. (2023). That's my tank on fire. *London Review of Books*, *45*(8). https://www.lrb.co.uk/the-paper/v45/n08/james-meek/that-s-my-tank-on-fire

Melnyk, A. (1996). Searle's abstract argument against strong AI. *Synthese*, *108*(3), 391–419.

Metz, C. (2000). Notes toward a phenomenology of the narrative. In M. McQuillan (Ed.), *The narrative reader* (pp. 86–91). London and New York: Routledge.

Microsoft. (2023). Eric Horvitz. https://www.microsoft.com/en-us/research/people/horvitz/

Miller, J. H. (2000). Line. In M. McQuillan (Ed.), *The narrative reader*. London and New York: Routledge.

Mitchell, M. C. (1984). Television and the Vietnam war. *Naval War College Review*, *37*(3), 42–52. http://www.jstor.org/stable/44636560

Moise, E. (2017). *The myths of Tet: The most misunderstood event of the Vietnam war*. Lawrence: University Press of Kansas.

Naughton, J. (2011, July 24). Thanks Marshall, I think we've finally got the message. *The Guardian*. https://www.theguardian.com/technology/2011/jul/24/marshall-mcluhan-media-john-naughton

NBC News. (2017, January 22). Kellyanne Conway: WH spokesman gave 'alternative facts' on inauguration crowd. https://www.nbcnews.com/storyline/meet-the-press-70-years/wh-spokesman-gave-alternative-facts-inauguration-crowd-n710466

Negroponte, N. (1995). *Being digital*. Cambridge, MA: MIT Press.

Nicholson, W. G. (1976). Teaching the new journalism. *The English Journal*, *65*(3), 55–57. https://doi.org/10.2307/814836

Nietzsche, F. (1996). *Human, all too human: A book for free spirits*. Cambridge: Cambridge University Press.

O'Brien, C. C. (1992). *The great melody: A thematic biography of Edmund Burke*. Chicago, IL: University of Chicago Press.

OECD. ((2019). OECD AI principles overview. https://oecd.ai/en/ai-principles

Ong, W. J. (1982). *Orality and literacy: The technologizing of the word*. London: Methuen & Co.

Ong, W. J. (1992). Writing is a technology that restructures thought. In P. A. Downing, S. D. Lima, & M. Noonan (Eds.), *The linguistics of literacy*. Amsterdam: John Benjamins.

O'Reilly, T. (2005, September 30). *What is web 2.0?: Design, patterns and business models for the next generation of software*. O'Reilly Network. http://www.oreilly.com/pub/a/web2/archive/what-is-web-20.html

Orwell, G. (2021). *Politics and the English language*. London: Renard Press.

Paine, T. (2012). *Common sense*. New York: Penguin.

Paine, T. (2018). *The rights of man*. Scotts Valley, CA: CreateSpace Independent Publishing Platform.

PBS. (2023). *Protests and backlash*. https://www.pbs.org/wgbh/americanexperience/features/two-days-in-october-student-antiwar-protests-and-backlash/

Pew. (2021, June 29). *Visit duration of newspaper websites*. Pew Research Center. https://www.pewresearch.org/journalism/chart/sotnm-newspapers-website-minutes-per-visit/

Pew. (2022, January 5). *Trust in America: Do Americans trust the news media?* Pew Research Center. https://www.pewresearch.org/2022/01/05/trust-in-america-do-americans-trust-the-news-media/

Pilger, J. (1989). *A secret country: The hidden Australia*. New York: Random House.

Polis. (2023). *Journalism and society*. Department of Media and Communications, London School of Economics. https://www.lse.ac.uk/media-and-communications/polis

Politkovskaya, A. (2003). *A small corner of Hell: Dispatches from Chechnya*. Chicago, IL: University of Chicago Press.

Polner, M. (1970). The underground GI press. *Columbia Journalism Review*, *9*(3), 54–56.

Polyák, G. (2019). Media in Hungary: Three pillars of an illiberal democracy. In E. Połońska & C. Beckett (Eds.), *Public service broadcasting and media systems in troubled European democracies* (pp. 279–303). London: Palgrave MacMillan.

Pomerantsev, P. (2019). *This is not propaganda: Adventures in the war against reality*. New York: Public Affairs.

Poole, S. (2019, December 25). From woke to gammon: Buzzwords by the people who coined them. *The Guardian*. https://www.theguardian.com/lifeandstyle/2019/dec/25/woke-to-gammon-buzzwords-by-people-coined-them

Postman, N. (1985). *Amusing ourselves to death: Public discourse in the age of show business*. New York: Viking Penguin.

Postman, N. (1992). *Technopoly: The surrender of culture to technology*. New York: Vintage.

Putnam, R. D. (2000). *Bowling alone: The collapse and revival of American community*. New York: Simon and Schuster.

Redmond, T. (2023). Office 365 reaches 345 million paid seats. https://office365itpros.com/2022/04/28/office-365-number-of-users/

Rheingold, H. (2000). *The Virtual community: Homesteading on the electronic frontier*. Cambridge, MA: MIT Press.

Robertson, R. (1992). *Globalization: Social theory and global culture*. London: Sage.

Rorty, R. (1989). *Contingency, irony, and solidarity*. Cambridge: Cambridge University Press.

Roszak, T. (1986). *The cult of information: The folklore of computers and the true art of thinking*. Cambridge, MA: Lutterworth Press.

Schiller, D. (2000). *Digital capitalism: Networking the global market system*. Cambridge, MA: MIT Press.

Schummer, J. (2001). Aristotle on technology and nature. *Philosophia Naturalis, 38*(1), 105–120.

Sennett, R. (2009). *The craftsman*. New York: Penguin.

Shannon, C. E. (1948). *The mathematical theory of communication*. Champaign: University of Illinois Press.

Shearer, E. (2021, January 12). *More than eight-in-ten Americans get news from digital devices*. Pew Research Center. https://www.pewresearch.org/short-reads/2021/01/12/more-than-eight-in-ten-americans-get-news-from-digital-devices/

Sheppard, R. Z. (1985, May 6). Awakening a sleeping giant the call. *TIME*. https://web.archive.org/web/20090508052211/http://www.time.com/time/magazine/article/0,9171,967544,00.html

Singer, A. (1983). The methods of form: On narrativity and social consciousness. *Substance, 41*, 64–77.

Snyder, T. (2018). *The road to unfreedom*. New York: Crown Publishing Group.

Srnicek, N. (2016). *Platform capitalism*. Cambridge, MA: Polity.

Srnicek, N. (2017). *Platform capitalism*. Cambridge, UK: Polity.

Sterne, J. (2016). Analog. In B. Peters (Ed.), *Digital keywords: A vocabulary of information society and culture* (pp. 31–44). Princeton, NJ: Princeton University Press.

Streeck, W. (2016). *How will capitalism end?* London: Verso.

Striphas, T. (2015). Algorithmic culture. *European Journal of Cultural Studies, 184*(4–5), 395–412.

Sunderland, A. (2019, December 12). A partiality for the truth. *Meanjin*. https://meanjin.com.au/blog/a-partiality-for-the-truth/

Tarnoff, B. (2022). *Internet for the people: The fight for our digital future*. London: Verso.

Terranova, T. (2004). *Network culture: Politics for the information age*. London: Pluto Press.

Tischler, B. L. (1990). Breaking ranks: GI antiwar newspapers and the culture of protest. *Vietnam Generation, 2*(1), 20–50.

Todorov, T. (2010). *In defense of the enlightenment*. London: Atlantic Books.

Turkle, S. (2017). *Alone together: Why we expect more from technology and less from each other*. New York: Basic Books.

UNESCO. (2017). What if we all governed the internet? https://unesdoc.unesco.org/ark:/48223/pf0000259717

U.S. Department of Defense. (2006). Office of Freedom of Information. https://sgp.fas.org/othergov/dod/embed.pdf

Van Doren, C. (1922, February 8). *The roving critic* (Vol. 114). New York: The Nation, p. 165.

Vaughan, B. J. (2020). War, media, and memory: American television news coverage of the Vietnam war. *Bridges: An Undergraduate Journal of Contemporary Connections*, *4*(1). https://scholars.wlu.ca/bridges_contemporary_connections/vol4/iss1/5

de Vaujany, F., & Mitev, N. (2017). The post-Macy paradox, information management and organizing: Good intentions and a road to hell? *Culture & Organization*, *23*(5), 379–407.

Virilio, P. (1995). *The art of the motor*. Minneapolis, MN: University of Minnesota Press.

Wark, M. (2021). *Capital is dead: Is this something worse?*. London: Verso.

Watzlawick, P. et al. (1967). *The pragmatics of human communication*. New York: W. W. Norton & Company.

Weber, M. (2005). *The protestant ethic and the spirit of capitalism*. London and New York: Routledge.

Weber, M. (2012). The 'objectivity' of knowledge in social science and social policy. In H. H. Bruun & S. Whimster (Eds.), *Max Weber: Collected methodological writings* (pp. 100–139). London: Routledge.

Wiener, N. (1954). *The human use of human beings*. New York: Houghton Mifflin.

Wilder, C. (1997). Being analog. In A. Berger (Ed.), *The postmodern presence* (pp, 239–253). London: Sage.

Williams, I. (2008). Plato: Media theorist. In P. Bounds & M. Jagmohan (Eds.), *Recharting media studies: Essays on neglected media critics* (pp. 21–54). New York: Peter Lang.

Williams, R. (1958). *Culture and society 1780–1950*. London: Chatto & Windus.

Williams, R. (1960). *Culture and society 1780–1950*. New York: Anchor Books.

Williams, R. (1961). *The long revolution*. London: Chatto & Windus.

Winner, L. (1980). Do artifacts have politics? *Daedalus*, *109*(1), 121–136. http://doi.org/10.2307/20024652

Winseck, D. (2011). The political economies of media and the transformation of the global media industries. In D. Winseck & D. Yong Jin (Eds.), *Political economies of media* (pp. 3–48). New York: Bloomsbury.

Wolf, M. (2007). *Proust and the squid: The story and science of the reading brain*. New York: Harper Perennial.

Wolf, M. (2018). *Reader, come home: The reading brain in a digital world*. New York: Harper Perennial.

Wolfe, T. (1973). *The new journalism*. New York: Harper and Row.

Wyatt, C. (2012, April 1). The Falklands for journalists: The ultimate embed experience. *BBC*. https://www.bbc.co.uk/blogs/collegeofjournalism/entries/5793e238-27a3-36bd-b63f-064717772aa7

Younge, G. (2013, July 23). Eduardo Galeano: 'My great fear is that we are all suffering from amnesia'. *The Guardian*. https://www.theguardian.com/books/2013/jul/23/eduardo-galeano-children-days-interview

Index

For Product Safety Concerns and Information please contact our EU representative GPSR@taylorandfrancis.com
Taylor & Francis Verlag GmbH, Kaufingerstraße 24, 80331 München, Germany

www.ingramcontent.com/pod-product-compliance
Lightning Source LLC
LaVergne TN
LVHW020642100826
845148LV00012B/2308

* 9 7 8 0 3 6 7 5 1 5 1 4 0 *